FATHERLESS

FATHERLESS

a memoir

KEITH MAILLARD

WEST VIRGINIA UNIVERSITY PRESS
MORGANTOWN 2019

ISBN
Paper 978-1-949199-13-0
Ebook 978-1-949199-14-7

Library of Congress Cataloging-in-Publication Data
Names: Maillard, Keith, 1942– author
Title: Fatherless : a memoir / Keith Maillard.
Description: First edition. | Morgantown : West Virginia University Press, 2019.
Identifiers: LCCN 2019010524| ISBN 9781949199130 (paperback) | ISBN
    9781949199147 (eBook)
Subjects: LCSH: Maillard, Keith, 1942– | Maillard, Keith, 1942—Family. | Authors,
    Canadian–Biography.
Classification: LCC PR9199.3.M345 Z46 2019 | DDC 813/.54 [B] –dc23
LC record available at https://lccn.loc.gov/2019010524

Book and cover design by Than Saffel / WVU Press
Cover image: Photograph of the author's father as a child, ca. 1909, probably taken
in Montreal. Courtesy of the author.

For my daughters
Jane and Elizabeth

This father is not even a shadow, not even a glance.
—Sartre

1.

I WAS IN MY OFFICE AT THE UNIVERSITY on an ordinary Monday morning—March 3, 1997—when I got the phone call, heard an unfamiliar man's voice asking if I was Keith Maillard. I said I was. "Are you related to Eugene Charles Maillard?"

If I were writing this as a scene in a novel, I would write in a beat here for myself—a significant pause while I tried to absorb the impact of the question—but I didn't hesitate at all. "Yes, that's my father."

"I'm sorry to have to tell you this, but your father has died."

I don't remember what I said—something to the effect of "Oh? Is that right?"

Later, when I would look at my agenda book, I would find that my right hand had taken off on its own and written "My father has died."

An outside observer would have seen my body sitting at my desk, functioning normally, making all the right noises into the telephone, but I didn't have a clue what I was feeling, and I can't describe it clearly now. "Squashed flat and pinned on a cold hard wall" is not bad, but that image is working too hard and doesn't get at the smeary unfocused blur of it. I could use psych jargon and call myself *depersonalized*, although that doesn't really do it either. I do remember exactly what I was thinking. What the hell

1

do you mean, he's *died*? Do you mean he's *just* died? How can that be? He was born in 1901, for Christ's sake. He must have been dead for years.

He died on the 25th of February, the voice was telling me—apparently this was my father's lawyer. My right hand continued to write down what he was saying. My father's funeral had been yesterday—a Masonic service conducted by my father's lodge in Escondido, California. My father had been cremated and his ashes scattered at sea. He'd been a remarkable man. He'd died just a few months short of his 96th birthday. He'd never lost his memory. He was lucid right up to the end.

"Oh, is that right?" I said. Why, I thought, should I give a shit whether or not he'd been lucid right up to the end?

The lawyer asked me for my address. He needed to send me legal documents. "I'm sorry to say that he didn't leave you anything."

"Uh-huh." Was I supposed to be surprised by that? Disappointed? If I'd known about my father's existence, I would have expected exactly what I'd always got from him—nothing.

I wrote down the lawyer's number, thanked him for calling. How strange, I thought—how meaningless and useless and anticlimactic. I'd never known my father, had never felt any personal connection to him, so it really shouldn't matter to me at all, but I seemed to be stuck at my desk. I had to find the next thing to do. I thought about a number of possibilities. I could cancel my class and go home, but that seemed melodramatic—a reaction out of all proportion to what had just happened—but what *had* just happened? Maybe nothing at all. Maybe I should just get on with my normal day. Or, if I was required to have an intense emotional reaction, I could go for a long walk. That's the way I've always coped with stress, but was this stress? What *was* I feeling? Maybe I wasn't feeling anything.

I called my wife, Mary, at work. She would tell me later that I sounded stunned and out of it. She asked me a series of perfectly logical questions. "How on earth did this lawyer find you?"

"I don't know."

"What do you mean you don't know? Didn't you ask him?"

"No."

"What did he tell you about your father?"

"I don't know. Not much of anything."

"Didn't you ask?"

None of this was making any sense. My father was dead. His funeral was yesterday. He was cremated and buried at sea. "Are you all right?" she said.

"Oh, sure. I'm fine."

She wanted the lawyer's phone number, and I gave it to her. I walked out of my office, rode the elevator down four floors, stepped outside into the perfectly ordinary gray overcast Vancouver day, and my feelings caught up to me.

My father hadn't appeared in my mind more than two or three times in the last ten years, so why was I so angry? And it wasn't just anger, it was honest-to-God fury—too big, too far gone for rational control—the kind of anger that could blot out the universe. I knew I had to keep moving. I didn't want to go striding off across campus headed for nowhere, so I paced back and forth in front of Buchanan—*my* building where I had a class scheduled in a little over an hour, where I would have to walk into the seminar room and impersonate not only a mature adult but a university professor. I was so angry I could see my own heartbeat in the sky. Of course I was talking to Gene Maillard, my dead father. "You son of a bitch. I spent my whole life not knowing a thing about you. You never gave me a thing. I tried to find you twice and got nowhere. You were absolutely elusive. You vanished into nothingness. And then, the day after your goddamned funeral, *you* can find *me* with no problem at all."

Everybody has to have a father even if that father has no more
human identity than a sperm cell. Did I always know that I had a
father? I think I did, but when I unpack my earliest memories, what
I find is a sense of things being "ordinary," and for me that meant
living with two women, my mother and grandmother. It took me
awhile to understand that other people thought "ordinary" meant
something else, so I didn't know that I was different until I met
other kids. They all seemed to have fathers. I learned to say what my
mother had taught me: "My parents are divorced." I learned to say
what I had decided for myself must be true: "Oh, it doesn't really
matter. I don't think about it at all."

Whenever I asked my mother about my father, what I heard
always sounded like a prerecorded message from the early days of
radio. It wasn't merely that the information never changed; the
words themselves never changed. "He was a good dancer," was the
first thing she said about him. "He was the cheapest man who ever
lived," was the second. The first was the reason she'd married him,
the second the reason she'd left him.

What kind of a dancer had he been? She didn't say. To illustrate
how cheap he'd been, she always told the same story. She and Gene
had been living in a distant city called "Hot Springs, Arkansas"—a
place of terrible magic and mystery to me as a child because
that's where they'd split up. I heard that terse, unchanging story
countless times—how it was a dreadfully hot day in Hot Springs,
Arkansas, and they were walking somewhere, my mother pushing
me in a baby carriage. She asked Gene for a nickel for a Coke. "Go
home and drink water," he said. "It's free."

Gene came from Canada, she told me. The men in his family
had been glassblowers. He was French from Alsace-Lorraine, and
he spoke French. He had wanted me to be named after him. If I
had been, I would have been the fourth Eugene, but she thought
that I deserved my own name. Gene had been out of town when

I was born. He'd called my mother in the hospital, asked, "How's Eugene?" My mother said, "His name's Keith," and he hung up on her.

That was pretty much everything I'd originally known about my father.

Like many people in our family, my mother could tell a good story in the grand old Appalachian tradition—could launch into a yarn with gusto, fill it up with fascinating details, answer endless questions about it, and tell it as many times as it needed to be told, and believe me, that was *many*. I grew up with her stories; they were as familiar to me as the Ohio River. I heard all about the Spanish flu, her friends in high school, the wonderful dances in the Lower Market, the grim days of the Depression. I even heard lots about that terrible place—Hot Springs, Arkansas—where her marriage had fallen apart. But about my father? If I tried to get her to add anything more to the flat, short, repetitive, closed-off statements she made about him, she'd say, "Oh, Keith, I don't remember." In her later years, she would say, "I don't *want* to remember."

As a child, I learned not to push her—it just made her angry and cold and distant—but sometimes, in spite of herself, she'd slip and say something new. I became watchful, alert for those unpredictable moments when I could snatch up another glittery fact to add to my precious small collection.

Once, when we were walking together—to church, I think— she stopped dead on the sidewalk, staring at me. "Good Lord," she said, "you walk just like him."

Another time she came home from town so rattled that she had to talk about what had just happened whether she wanted to or not. She'd been having a sandwich at the five-and-dime, had heard a woman at the other end of the lunch counter saying, "Yes, his name's Eugene Maillard. He lived with his sister."

I couldn't understand why that bothered her. She didn't seem to understand it either. All she could say was "I don't know, honey. It didn't feel right. *People I didn't know* talking about Gene and Olga." That was the first I'd heard any mention of my father's sister. Someone who had to be *my aunt*. If I had an Aunt Olga, maybe I had other relatives, but if I did, I'd never heard a word about them.

My absent father had always been a black hole in my life—no matter what I directed into it, nothing ever came out of it—and by this point he certainly shouldn't have mattered a damn to me. I was, after all, no longer a six-year-old. I was a responsible adult halfway through his fifties, a family man, a published novelist, a respected teacher, a property owner. I had the world's greatest job. I had succeeded, as the cliché would have it, beyond my wildest dreams—or, as I liked to put it, "I'm doing pretty good for a poor boy from West Virginia"—and I had succeeded without a father, without even thinking about him very much. Not only that, but I had succeeded *in spite of him*—because people with fathers learn certain essential life skills far more quickly than I had, with a hell of a lot less fuss, and not having a father had presented me, right from the start, with a set of demonic puzzles it had taken me years to solve. Everything I'd done, I'd done without him, so why should it matter to me that this unknown man—Eugene Charles Maillard, my biological father—had just died. But it did matter. I could tell how much it mattered by how angry I was.

The first time I tried to find my father, I was in my early twenties, studying philosophy at West Virginia University with a cheery old gent named William Minor who professed his own wildly optimistic variety of John Dewey pragmatism and believed that all moral, social, and political problems could be solved by rational thought. He taught us to take the same set of tools that we applied to the big issues and apply them to ourselves—that is, we could use philosophy to think our way through the twists and turns of our own lives; all we had to do was define our terms, correlate our means and ends, and proceeded logically, step by step. He offered "conferences" for any of us who wanted to work with him on our personal problems, and I took him up on it.

I don't remember how the issue of my father came up—although it would have been astonishing if it hadn't—and I told Professor Minor the same story I always told everybody. I knew nothing about my father and didn't care to know anything. Being fatherless hadn't meant a thing to me. I'd done just fine without a father, and I was going to go on doing just fine without a father, thank you very much. Professor Minor did not believe me. After I sat in his office for a few minutes and thought about it—logically, step by step—I didn't believe myself either.

All the time I was growing up, we received a check in the mail once a month—a check for twenty-two dollars—and that was the only contact I'd ever had with my father. There was never anything besides the check—never a query as to how I was doing, never a personal note, not even a few words scribbled onto a card. My mother made sure I knew that the only reason Gene sent us even that little bit of money was because the court made him do it—he would certainly never have done it on his own because he was *the cheapest man who ever lived*. We received the last check in February 1960, because I'd turned eighteen on the 28th of that month, and "to his eighteenth birthday" was all the court had ordered. Gene could have sent me a birthday card with that last check, or a note saying, "Welcome to manhood," or even "Happy birthday," but he didn't. The last check was the last check.

Those checks had to have been mailed from *somewhere*, and I asked my mother for Gene's address. She did not give it to me graciously. She dug through her old papers, found the address, wrote it out, and slapped it down with the air of "All right, you asked for it, so there you are, and now be damned with you."

I can't remember what I wrote to my father. I do remember that my letter radiated ambivalence out of every sentence. The long and the short of it went something like this: "You probably don't want to hear from me or know anything about me, but in case you do, here's my address." I remember thinking that the burden was on him, the adult who had vanished and left me behind, and if he wanted to get to know me, he should make some effort, because I was, after all, making the effort of writing that letter—however double-faced, surly, and resentful it might be—so the onus was on him to write back and open up some line of communication that might eventually lead us into a genuine conversation. I mailed the letter and received exactly what I'd always got from him—nothing.

The second time I tried to find my father was some twenty years later. After I'd emigrated to Canada in 1970, my life, like the universe, had been unfolding as it should—indeed with a good deal of success—but then, in the early 1980s, I seemed to have fallen into a pit, the deep-shit abysm, the soggy bottom of the Dixie Cup. I was a writer with writer's block, a middle-aged goof going nowhere fast, a man who was in between books, in between jobs, in between relationships—in between everything. If there was a next step forward out of that pit—even a small step—I couldn't see it. A friend recommended a therapy group in Seattle; their work was supposed to be very fast and very effective—just what I needed—so I rode the bus down to Seattle for a "three-day intensive."

The method employed by that particular therapy group was to shove you directly into whatever was making you feel bad and keep you there until you cried about it. It sounds simple-minded, but it does work. If you tell the story of your life and cry about all the things that really matter, and if you cry for three days straight while sympathetic people hand you Kleenex and urge you to cry some more, you're almost sure to feel better afterward, and I did.

Of course my father came up. I said all of the same things I'd said to Professor Minor, practically verbatim: "Know nothing about him—blah, blah, blah. Don't care—blah, blah, blah. Doesn't really matter—blah, blah, blah." The therapist in Seattle didn't believe me any more than Professor Minor had. "Where does your father live?" she asked me.

I couldn't remember exactly where I'd sent my unanswered letter so many years ago. I hadn't saved the address. "Washington State somewhere," I said. "I think he might even live in Seattle."

The therapist gave me a look so heavy I could have anchored a freighter to it. "Do you think it's an accident that you're in Seattle *right now*?"

I don't know what I thought. My father was a draftsman, and my mother had always told me that he worked for Sanderson & Porter. The therapist pointed at the phone in the next room. It turned out that Sanderson & Porter did have an office in Seattle, and I called it. Someone told me that, yes, Eugene Maillard had worked there, but he'd been transferred to the San Francisco office a number of years ago. When I got back to Vancouver, I called the San Francisco office. They told me that I must have been misinformed. No one named Eugene Maillard had ever worked for them.

Maybe it was the three-day intensive, or maybe it was just time for something to change for the better, so I took the next step, and the next step after that. I could have kept up my search for my father, I suppose, gone through phone directories, called the Seattle office back and said, "Who was it who told me that Eugene Maillard used to work there? Do you actually have *a record* of Eugene Maillard working there?" But the way I'd always dealt with my father made an old and comfortable groove in my mind, and I slid back into it—I didn't think about him much. Besides, I'd met him in Seattle—he'd appeared in the therapist's empty chair—and we'd cried together. I'd told him how much I'd missed having him around when I was a kid, and I'd given him signed copies of the books I'd written. He'd told me how sorry he was that he hadn't been around and how much he'd missed me. We'd hugged each other and cried some more. Of course I'd been making him up, but that was nothing new—I'd been making him up my whole life.

Mary, my wife, is a documentary editor and a genealogist. From her grandfather, the colonel, she inherited a copy of a chart of her father's side of the family—an elaborate document that stands in a corner of her office rolled up like a papyrus. When she spreads it out on the dining room table, it looks nothing like a conventional family tree; if you didn't know what it was, you might take it for a schematic diagram of the electrical power grid for the entire Eastern Seaboard of the United States. At the intersections of innumerable, bewildering, densely tangled lines are little dots, and each dot is a unique person who once had a history and a life. For Mary, it's not good enough to know merely the name that goes with the dot; she wants to know *the whole story* because she's connected to that dot *by blood*. After years of research, Mary has learned the whole stories that go with an astonishingly large number of those dots.

When I got home from school that night, Mary was waiting to pounce on me. She was hoping that now she could do what she'd always wanted—draw a genealogical chart for the Maillards and learn *their* stories. She'd called the lawyer in California and had a long chat with him, asking him all the questions I'd been too stunned to ask.

"How the hell did they find me?" I wanted to know.

"Oh," she said, "that's an interesting story."

Gene had taught dance and music for years. His best student—Kippy—had become a professional harp player, and she'd played at Gene's funeral. People were talking after the service, and somebody said, "It's too bad Gene didn't have any family," and Kippy said, "Oh, he does have a son. He's a writer in Canada," so Tom—that was the lawyer. *Tom.* By the end of the phone call, Mary and Tom were on a first-name basis—so Tom thought, okay, if he's a writer, maybe he's published a book. He went to the Escondido Public Library and discovered that not only had I published a book, I'd published several—they even had some of them right there on the shelf—and Tom picked one up, turned it over, saw my picture, and knew instantly that I was Gene's son. The dust jacket said that I taught at the University of British Columbia, so he called UBC and got my office number. It was that simple.

"He didn't have any other children," Mary said.

The last time we'd visited my mother in West Virginia, Mary had got more information out of her than I had in nearly fifty years of covert operations. "Was Gene ever married before?" she'd asked in her most innocent Little Mary Sunshine voice, and without a flicker of hesitation, my mother had said, "Oh, yes. Twice."

"Did he have any other kids?"

"Oh, yes. I think he did . . . I don't remember. I think he had two boys."

Mary had been delighted. She'd imagined my elder brothers floating around out there somewhere in the world waiting for me to find them, and of course there was also the possibility that Gene had married again, so I might have any number of siblings, running loose and undiscovered—leading, in Mary's happy fantasies, to a series of touching reunions, to more warmly human stories to add to the genealogical collection. I'd never been that optimistic. I wasn't at all sure that lost Maillards wanted to be found—or, more to the point, that *I* wanted to find them—but now I was just as disappointed as Mary to see them vanish.

She'd asked Tom if he was sure, and he was. It was a legal matter. In order to make Gene's will, he had to know. "And Gene

was quite definite about it," she said. "He only had one child, and
you're it."

Tom had given Mary the phone number of the executor of
Gene's estate, a guy named Gus Klammer. "Call him," Mary said.

"I'm still kind of out of it, OK?"

We looked at each other, deadlocked. She shrugged—have it
your way. "He was a tap dancer," she said.

"Who? Gene?" *Of course he was a tap dancer*, I thought,
although that was the first I'd ever heard of it.

"Call Gus."

"Yeah, yeah," I said, "I'll call him." I'll call him in a while. I'll
call him after dinner. I'll call him *later.* "Give me a break," I said.
"I'm having trouble processing this shit." I walked outside and
paced in a circle in front of my house. I do that a lot. Wherever I
live, I always wear down a circular groove in the lawn.

At that time, we lived in an odd split-level house built in the
early fifties. We'd bought it on a fluke. Vancouver housing prices
hardly ever do anything but go up, but there'd been a brief slump,
a period of about six months in which nobody had been buying a
damned thing, so we'd made a low-ball offer, and, to our shock, it
had been accepted. Now we were mortgaged up to our eyeballs,
but we were, nonetheless, homeowners. I loved walking around
our queer five-sided lot, admiring our lavender, thyme, and roses,
admiring our peculiar house and its peculiar features—the cedar
deck gone blue in the rain, the sliding glass doors that opened onto
a sunken patio, the ancient shakes disintegrating on the roof. As
wildly improbable as it would seem given the first half of my life,
I was happily married and lived a quiet life in a nice home with
my wife and two daughters—and I liked using precisely those
bland, colorless, uninformative words to tell myself my own story.
I *wanted* my life to be happy, quiet, and nice, and it was—but it

never stopped feeling strange to me. How did I get there? I liked walking around outside thinking how strange it was. I wanted to remember, always, where I'd come from.

My thirteen-year-old daughter Jane was over on Erwin Drive that night, playing with her two best girl friends in a bit of woods where they'd created a fantasy land and peopled it with their own creations. I am not her biological father, but I'm her dad and have been ever since she was four. By genetic coincidence Jane and I look enough alike that people meeting us for the first time usually assume that we're related, and that pleases both of us. Despite the recent appearance of street-sweeper jeans and Goth makeup, Jane was still a dreamy little girl, and that was just fine with me.

My other daughter, Elizabeth, was seven. She carries my genes, and I've always recognized in her a stubborn, quirky, idiosyncratic streak that feels like it came straight from me. She hardly ever does anything that she doesn't want to do. I'd picked her up that day, as I did most week days, from the dance school where she was doing what she *did* want to do—ballet, jazz, and tap. The best I could tell, she'd always thought of herself as a dancer. Lately Elizabeth was refusing to acknowledge herself by the name her parents preferred, so *Liz*, at that moment, was in her room in the basement waiting to be called for dinner, watching a kid's show on television and braiding a bracelet, or a necklace, or just a long hunk of braid that had no use whatsoever. She braided things for hours. When she ran out of the yarn we bought her, she braided dental floss. And my wife? She was sitting inside at the kitchen table fuming at me for not calling my father's executor in California.

Just as I'd told Mary, things *were* happening too fast for me. I *was* having trouble processing them. "He was a good dancer"— that was the core of the myth about my father; every other fantasy I'd created about him had been built around that undefined core. He came from Canada and spoke French, so of course he'd been a good dancer—in my child's mind it came with the territory—but I'd always thought that my mother must have meant *a social dancer*, someone who'd squired her around a ballroom in a convincing way. I saw him in a tuxedo in a 1930s movie; he was in a New York penthouse sipping champagne. Later I saw him wearing a captain's uniform, or maybe a major's, my mother in a herringbone suit, in mules with white socks because you couldn't buy stockings during the war. I saw them in black-and-white newsreels as battleships fired off their guns, or bombs fell from open bays, smashing cities. I saw *The Best Years of Our Lives* when I was five. Were those the best years of their lives? I always saw them dancing forever in that living, glowing, vividly charged, unbearably poignant black-and-white movie that had been playing just before I'd been born.

I wasn't quite ready to let go of that story; I'd poured too much energy into it until it had grown its own cheesy beauty, but now it seemed that I was going to have to rewrite it. I'd never imagined Gene as *a tap dancer*, but it made perfect sense the moment I'd heard it. It fell into place with the clang of inevitability, but it also flipped things into a new pattern.

When she'd been six, Liz had watched a documentary on Shirley Temple, a two-hour show that began with a child actress younger than Liz herself and then followed Shirley on through adolescence and into adulthood. I'd never seen Liz grabbed by anything quite the way that show grabbed her; she watched it as though the events were unfolding in real time right before her eyes. Whenever there was a commercial break, she ran upstairs to give me a blow-by-blow account. Incensed on Shirley's behalf, she followed me around the kitchen saying, "They're being really mean to her. Why are they doing that, Dad? They won't put her in any more movies." She watched the entire show, far beyond the point when I would have expected her to run out of interest. Why should she care that Shirley had grown up and become an ambassador?

But she seemed to care, and somewhere along the way, she must have decided either that she was very much like Shirley, or, maybe, that she *was* Shirley.

Liz asked for a Shirley Temple video, so we bought her two of them. She asked for more, so we bought her all of them. She was already taking tap, and we thought that her obsession was simply an extension of that. She would watch the videos, isolate the tap routines, and play them over and over, trying to imitate Shirley's steps. She wanted to be Shirley in a Kiwanis competition, so we arranged for a few private lessons with her tap teacher. She learned "At the Codfish Ball," the song and dance routine from *Captain January*. We improvised a costume, had her already curly hair set into ringlets—I have a picture of her in the beautician's chair with a copy of *Child Star* on her lap. She didn't win first place, but she finished in the money.

"If I met Shirley," Liz asked me, "do you think she'd know who I am?"

Liz was not only my daughter but Gene's *granddaughter*. What did I know about recent discoveries in genetics? Nothing. But I had grown up saturated with the old West Virginia notions of blood and kinship, and that way of looking at the world still resonated with me. Now I felt sure that my daughter had inherited her love of dance from Gene.

2.

WE ATE DINNER, AND I CLEANED UP THE KITCHEN. Mary kept saying, "Call him, call him, call him," but I was running into an ancient bedrock of resistance, a wordless lump inside me as thick and unresponsive as mud. If I tried to turn what I was feeling into words, it would probably come out as that witless old saw "let sleeping dogs lie," and I knew better than to try that one on my wife. It was all just too damned much—all just leftover childhood crap—all too familiar. Some big part of me still didn't want to know anything about my father.

As a delaying tactic, I laid out on the bed table everything I would need—methodically—telephone, notebook, reading glasses, several pens. I drew up a chair. Mary was sitting on the edge of the bed waiting for me to get on with it. I dialed. Gus Klammer answered immediately.

Gus wasn't hard to talk to—quite the opposite. He loved talking about Gene. I took excellent notes. Reading them now, I can see that I must have jotted down a shorthand version of nearly everything he said. While I was doing it, I again had the sense of running on autopilot. I was, by God, going to do everything right this time. I was, by God, going to impersonate a normal human being, someone who gave a shit. I told Gus about trying to find my

father and running into a dead end. It seemed sad and bitter that
when I did find him, he'd just died.

It *was* sad, Gus said. He couldn't have been more sympathetic.
He told me the story I'd already heard—about the funeral and
the harp player, Kippy. She was Gene's favorite student, a former
beauty queen, a professional musician. She'd known Gene really
well, and she'd be glad to talk to me. He gave me her number.

Gus had the confident, booming, upbeat voice of one of
those old guys—they seem to abound in Masonic circles—who,
when you ask them how they're doing, invariable reply, "Terrific!
Couldn't be better!"—and mean it. He was also a bit hard of
hearing. At the top of the first page in my notebook, I wrote "old"
for Mary to see and drew a ring around it.

"Gene was a very thrifty man," Gus said. "You could call him
tight."

Ah, there was the man I knew, the man of the legend—*the
cheapest man who ever lived*. I wrote "tight" for Mary, and we
grinned at each other.

The Masonic lodge was at the center of everything, Gus told
me. He and Gene were both members of the one in Escondido;
that's how they'd met. Gene had given up driving, and he'd needed
rides to doctors' appointments. Gus volunteered to take him. The
first time Gus picked him up, Gene complained about another
Masonic brother: "He always wanted *a little something* for the gas
tank." Then he said to Gus—pointedly—"Well, I expect you'll
want a little something for the gas tank too?"

"No, Gene," Gus told him, "I don't want anything for the gas
tank. I'm doing this *for you*." After that, they'd been the best of
friends.

My first page of notes is little more than a listing of facts.
The information was coming out in no particular order, and

that's the way I wrote it down. Gene had a business card that said "entertainer." He'd weighed about a hundred and twenty-five pounds—no, not a big man at all, a lean, small, wiry man, "a working fool." Gene had retired from General Electric in Washington state, where he'd worked for years. He'd come to Escondido for his health—he always had allergies and other health problems. He'd motored from Washington to California in an old Oldsmobile.

Gene never had too much help from his family. Everything he'd got in his life, he'd got on his own. When he'd been a kid, Gene had taught himself to tap dance; later on, he'd taught himself music. He worked his way through college playing in a band and teaching tap dancing. He taught himself to play the piano, and he played in the big bands back in Chicago and Philly in the 20s and 30s. He made his money by running two dance schools and two music schools. He always had a regular job—worked as an engineer draftsman, designed equipment for General Electric— and he took all the money he made from his dance schools and music schools and put it into life insurance annuities. By the time he was in his eighties, all of them were paying off. He was a wealthy man. He'd donated a lot of money to Masonic charities.

Mary wrote in the margin with her red pen, "Ask him about himself," so I did. Gus told me that he'd been born in Alberta. What an odd coincidence, I thought, another Canadian. He was retired, he said. His wife had died in 1990, and now most of his time was taken up by Masonic activities. But he didn't want to talk about himself; he wanted to talk about my father.

Gene was "an unusual man," Gus said—tight and thrifty. He didn't own a good suit or a good pair of pants, wore the same old suit for years and watched every penny. He had bad eyes; that's why he was interested in the eye foundation where'd he left his money. He'd first joined the Masons in 1925 in Pittsburgh.

He belonged to five Masonic lodges and held life memberships in all of them. He wore thick glasses, but he loved to read; he read *Reader's Digest* every month. In his last years, he'd had a colostomy. He only weighed ninety or ninety-five pounds when he died.

It was unfortunate, Gus said, but not too many Freemasons visited Gene in his last days. Just before he died, Gene said to Gus, "I think it's time now. You stay right here. You stay all night," but Gus hadn't been able to do that. He had things he had to do back in town. He was sorry he hadn't been there.

Then, with the tone of someone reciting confidently from a report, Gus rattled off a series of numbers: "Gene was born on May the second, 1901. When he died, he was ninety-five and ten and a half months old. He died at seven minutes to six in the evening on Tuesday." It took me a moment to get the significance of what I'd just heard—it was Gus Klammer in his official role as the executor, making his report to Keith Maillard, *Gene's son*.

Over the years Gene had donated huge amounts of money to the lodge in Escondido, but he didn't feel appreciated. He complained to Gus, "Well, they bought me dinner, but that's all they ever did," so Gus had an oil painting done of Gene and hung it in the lodge. Gus paid for it himself.

Gene told Gus a lot about his unhappy childhood. An older half-brother and a cousin had mistreated Gene terribly. Once, they'd been sitting in an open second-story window, waiting for him to come home from school. Gene had looked up and seen them sitting there, laughing at him. When he came in the house and went upstairs, they grabbed him and threw him out the window. Another time they heated a steel bar in a fire and made him carry it. His hands were so badly burned that his mother kept his hands wrapped in buttermilk and fresh butter for two weeks. Gene couldn't tell on the boys because they'd threatened to kill him if he did. Gene's father died young. When his mother passed away, Gene disowned the rest of his family.

My father had been married three times, and divorced three times, and glad of it every time. He loved talking about his last divorce. On the day it was finalized, he went into the Elks Club with a little cake he'd bought in a local bakery—a cupcake about four inches wide. He had a candle in his pocket. He sat in the back corner of the Elks Club all by himself, shoved the candle into the cake and lit it. Some people came over and said, "What's up, Gene? Is it your birthday?"

"No," he said, "it's my divorce day." They asked him if he wanted to have a divorce party, and he said, "Yes, I do."

To the tune of "Happy Birthday," they sang "Happy Divorce Day." He said, "Make sure you sing 'divorce.'" They said, "Well, seeing as it's your divorce day, everything's on the house, everything's free," so Gene drank and feasted all by himself at the Elks Club, and eventually it filled up with people, and they kept singing, "Happy divorce day to you," and Gene kept saying, "Don't forget 'divorce.' Make sure you put in the word 'divorce.'" He was so loaded by the end of the night that somebody had to help him home to bed.

That story made things uncomfortably real for me. I knew what an Elks Club was like because my uncle Bill used to take me, my mother, and my cousins to the one in Wheeling—I could picture the scene clearly—and that was the divorce from *my mother* Gene had been celebrating. I could understand how my mother might drive a man nuts—she'd driven me nuts on more than one occasion—so I could sympathize with him up to a point, feel something of his glee, but what had he felt about losing me?

Gus asked if I wanted any of Gene's personal effects, and I said I did. Was there anything in particular? I asked him if my father had a pair of tap shoes, and he said of course he did, and I could certainly have them. Maybe I would like to have my father's scrapbooks too? All my psychic antennae pricked up. What scrapbooks?

Gene had documented his career in two scrapbooks. He always told Gus that they were the most valuable things he owned— that his whole life was in those scrapbooks. In his last years, as he was moving from his apartment to a senior citizens home, and from there to a nursing home, he always asked, "Where are the scrapbooks, Gus? You've got to make sure they're safe." I told Gus that, yes, I wanted those scrapbooks. I wanted them very much.

Gene had never mentioned having a son until he'd had to make his will in his early nineties, so Gus had been surprised to hear about me. He asked Gene if he'd made any attempt to stay in touch. Gene said he'd tried, but the problem was "the mother-in-law." The last time he'd seen me had been when I was about three. He came to visit us in Wheeling, brought me a ball, sat down on the floor with me. He rolled the ball to me, and I rolled it back. I was talking by then, and he could see that I was a bright little boy, and we were getting along just fine, but all the time he was there, *the mother-in-law* was standing in the doorway with a carving knife in one hand and a sharpening stone in the other, carefully and slowly and methodically sharpening the knife.

Gene said that the mother-in-law was a truly frightening lady— the main reason he didn't maintain contact with me. The mother-in-law had never liked him, and he could never get through the barriers she put up. She'd been a key factor in the breakup of the marriage.

That story made things more than merely real—I could see it so clearly, I could have directed it for the screen. "The mother-in-law" was my grandmother, the woman who'd raised me. I still own the knife she was sharpening—and the stone too. Over the years, that stone has been worn down to a slender, pencil-sized nubbin, just as that carving knife has been worn down to a thin sliver of a scimitar-shaped blade.

I saw my grandmother sharpening that knife countless times. Her hands always had to be busy. When she wasn't cooking or cleaning up, she knitted or crocheted, but she never simply sat still. Sharpening that knife might have been reflexive. She might not have been aware of how threatening she looked to Gene— or maybe she had done it intentionally to send him a message. She was perfectly capable of something like that. I could see her standing there in the doorway, watching, listening—could hear the steady scrape, scrape, scrape of the steel on the stone. If she hadn't liked Gene, he would have known it.

As we were coming to the end of the conversation, I heard Gus move into the rhetoric of summation. He was, after all, the one who'd delivered the eulogy at Gene's funeral, and now I heard him saying those things that one is called upon to say when a life is over and one needs to find the proper words to close it out. Gene was an unusual man. He'd never held any office in any order, but he'd been active in the Masons, going up thirty-two degrees in both the Scottish and the York Rites and finally becoming a Shriner. In seventy-two years, he'd never been president or master of any lodge, but he'd always entertained on social nights. He'd done skits, recited poems and verses, sung songs, danced. Yes, he was an unusual man. He was an entertainer.

He worked hard. He taught his dance and music classes. He was tight. He hung onto every penny, and he gave to charity. When Gene was in his last years and he was making up his will, Gus asked him if he might want to see his son. "You know, we could probably find him for you."

Gene was old and feeble by then. He said, "I wouldn't want him to see me like this."

Whatever I was feeling, I was going to have to deal with it later. I still had another phone call to make—to Kippy, Gene's best student. I knew that if I didn't call her now, I might never call her at all.

The notes from our conversation fill hardly a page, but everything she said counted for something. Gus had primarily been giving me information, but Kippy seemed more concerned with feelings—hers, Gene's, mine. What was essential happened beneath the words and didn't lend itself to shorthand transcription. Much of the time I simply listened to her. She had a voice like fine silk—a warmly empathetic voice that drew me in and made me trust her, trust everything she said.

Gene had worked with Kippy's father at the Hanford atomic energy plant in Richland, Washington. *Atomic energy plant*? I thought. OK, that was something else I would have to deal with later.

Gene had taught Kippy to tap dance back in the 50s when she'd been growing up. She remembered doing a dance routine on a drum, and she also remembered a wonderful soft shoe number that Gene had taught her. If she concentrated, she could probably still do it. She had won the Miss Tri-Cities and the Miss Washington pageants, had been a contestant in the Miss America pageant. She was a professional harpist and had played for twenty years at the Dunes in Las Vegas. After Gene retired from the GE plant in Richland, he moved to Escondido. He visited Kippy in Las Vegas and heard her play.

Gene knew that I was an author in Canada, and she asked him once—they'd been walking together; she remembered that—and she asked him if he wanted her to try to find me. He didn't answer immediately. He was very hesitant. She could sense a pain there. And he said, no, he didn't think so, and she pressed a bit and said,

"Well, maybe I should just go and find him anyway," and he said, "Don't you dare!"

She thought at the time that she shouldn't interfere in something she didn't know anything about, but now she regretted it. Now she thought that Gene, in his last years, might have wanted to meet me, get to know me, but was afraid of a possible rejection. He didn't know whether I'd want to know him or not.

Gene had always told her that he'd had an unhappy childhood. No, it hadn't been a good family to grow up in. His older half-sister, Olga, had taken him to dances, and that's how he'd learned to dance. Olga hadn't been allowed to go unless she took Gene with her. He'd danced with all of Olga's girlfriends too.

When he was in his eighties living in Escondido, he got up early every day and tap danced for twenty minutes; then he played his marimba. He wanted to keep in practice, stay in shape. He entertained at old folks homes, did skits—things like "The Night Before Christmas"—and his song and dance routines. "We've got to brighten up the old folks," he said. At Christmas, she'd known that he wasn't going to be around too much longer, that he was about ready to go.

Kippy went in to see him just a few days before he died. He couldn't talk, but she sensed that he knew who she was. One night she had the feeling that she had to go back, so she took her harp with her, set it up in his room, and played for him. She played the old tap dance songs they used to do when she'd been Gene's student. She played "Tea for Two," one of their old standards. He tried to say something to her but couldn't. She said, "Remember this, Gene? Remember when we danced to this? Remember when you taught me to dance?"

3.

I'D LEARNED MORE ABOUT MY FATHER in those two phone calls than I'd known in fifty years. Everything I'd heard had been both surprising and not surprising at all. I'd been touched by the stories I'd heard about Gene, but that was somehow beside the point. Accounts of anyone's death can be moving, but they're much more moving if you know the person, and I hadn't known him. We'd just missed each other. He might as well have been dead years ago, just as I'd imagined. Now I'd never get to meet him or talk to him, so what did that leave me? An interesting research project?

Yes, it was all *interesting*, all *material*, but material for what? It made me uneasy. I even sensed that it might turn out to be dangerous to me, as radioactive as Hanford. What had my father been doing at an atomic energy plant anyway? I kept seeing cartoon images of Homer Simpson juggling glowing bars of plutonium.

I knew I'd feel more comfortable if I could fall back into my old habitual default position—no, I never knew my father, and it didn't matter much—but I couldn't quite get there. If somebody had to emerge out of nothingness to assume the shape of my father, Gene seemed like a pretty good candidate. Everything I'd heard about him so far had made me like him. I was even beginning to feel connected to him.

Our friend Fari told us that we should make a shrine for my
father the way she would have done back home in Iran. I was Gene's
only son, she said, so his soul would have come shooting straight
to our home the moment he died, and we should make sure he felt
welcome. The ritual appealed to the unreconstructed mystic in me,
and I thought, too, that it would be a colorful way to introduce
Liz to her grandfather. Fari said we needed a picture of Gene and
something that had belonged to him. When she'd left him, my
mother had destroyed every picture, every document, every scrap of
evidence that Gene had ever existed, but she'd spared one snapshot,
maybe because her brother and her uncle were in it too. As soon as
I'd found that picture, I'd whisked it away and saved it. And, yes,
I did own something that had belonged to my father; it was the
only thing of his I owned. I couldn't remember why my mother
had given it to me. I must have been asking questions again—the
ones that she didn't want to answer. She'd rummaged in a kitchen
drawer, handed me a perfectly ordinary kitchen knife. "Well, here
it is," she'd said in the clipped, bitter voice she used whenever she
talked about my father, "all that's left of my marriage."

A little dirty black-and-white picture and an old kitchen knife
might not have been much, but they were enough for Fari. She
built a shrine on the fireplace down in Elizabeth's room, set out
rosewater from Persia in front of it, a bowl of wet pudding that she
called "halva," and a vase of roses. She lit half a dozen candles. We
had to maintain this shrine for three days, she said. The candles
must never be allowed to go out, had to burn down until they were
finished. These were gifts for my father's soul. "We pray for him,"
she said, "thanks Mohammed."

I'd rediscovered my father's knife in a carton labeled "family
stuff"—a repository for old papers and photographs my mother

had given me over the years. Maybe, I thought, she hadn't destroyed *every* scrap of evidence about my father. What I found there was exactly what I'd expected—a massive collection of material from her family and nothing about my father—but then, near the bottom, there was a little book called *Family Tree*, a bit of kitsch my mother must have bought in a five-and-dime. A drawing of a tree ran up in the middle of the page, its branches—decorated with pale blue blossoms—spread out across the top and supported a pale pink hammock with a silly rosy-cheeked baby in it. The right side had boxes for the mother's family, the left for the father's, and my mother had filled them in. My father's place of birth was listed as Coraopolis, Pennsylvania. That couldn't be right. She'd always told me he was born in Canada.

"Maybe they came to Canada first," Mary said.

"Yeah," I said. There had to be a Canadian connection—my mother had said it far too clearly far too many times for there not to be one. I'd grown up thinking of Canada as a second home. I'd felt half Canadian before I'd ever come here. "Glassblowers from France," I said. "They came from Alsace-Lorraine and lived in Montreal. That was her standard line."

My grandparents' names were listed there too. It was the first time I'd ever seen them. My mother's clear bookkeeper's handwriting had been replaced by somebody else's, a smaller, less-legible script. She must have asked *my father* to enter those names. I felt my skin prickle. That was actually *his handwriting*—and if my father had entered those names, they had to be right. My grandfather was not, as I'd expected, another Eugene Charles Maillard, but Eugene Francois Maillard. He'd been born exactly where my mother had always told me—Lyon. My grandmother, Clementine Mariani, had been born in Parma, France. Weird, I thought. *France*? The last I heard, Parma was in Italy.

The first of many packages from Gus Klammer arrived. I'd never before felt the full force of the phrase "last effects." Here were all the sad, intensely personal objects a dead man leaves behind, things that are of no conceivable use to anyone else. Gene's wallet was in there—an old, worn, black, flattened leather relic—and his glasses, his medical prescriptions, a dozen or so business cards, random scraps of papers with phone numbers written on them—as though Gus had gathered up everything lying around on Gene's bed table and stuffed it into a box.

Liz and I had an appointment to get our eyes examined. I was halfway to the car when I remembered that Gene had bad eyes. I went back to get his glasses so our doctor could compare our prescriptions. "Amazing," he said, "look at this." The degrees of myopia and astigmatism in me, Gene, and Liz were remarkably similar. And in all of us, our left eye was worse than our right. There, expressed in numbers, I saw my father's genes flowing down to us.

From the moment I'd first seen that picture I'd stolen from my mother, I'd known that I looked like Gene. I had his brown eyes and his allergies, and so did his granddaughter. But the connection I felt went deeper than physical characteristics. In my old family notion of blood, you didn't just inherit the color of your eyes; you inherited whole chunks of your personality.

The notion of a "self-made man" has always bothered me. If I wrote down the names of the people who've helped me over the years, the list would go on for pages, but in the way the term is generally used, I suppose I could say that I'm self-made—just like my father. I too was a self-taught musician—and had taught music—but, more importantly, I was a self-taught novelist, good enough at writing that I'd been hired by a university to teach other people how to do it. It was the best possible job for me—I taught what I did, and I did what I taught. My students were getting published, building careers. I was a success, and I'd got there on my own—just like my father.

I was beginning to recognize in Gene a set of characteristics, a quality of personality, that was mine too, that I thought I could also see emerging in my daughter—an unlikely combination of self-directed maverick and intensely social team player—but I still hadn't got to the bottom of it. I could feel a connection with Gene that was deeper than anything I could articulate. Finding out about him was like finding missing pieces of myself. Already I felt I could claim him, say, "Yes, I *did* have a father."

A few days later, Gene's will arrived in the mail. If anyone had told me that I would be upset by reading it, I would have said, "Oh, no, why would I be upset?" I'd thought that I would just read it, find it interesting, and put it away in a file. That isn't what happened.

Last Will and Testament
of
EUGENE C. MAILLARD

I, EUGENE C. MAILLARD, also known as EUGENE CHARLES MAILLARD, also known as GENE MAILLARD, a resident of Escondido, San Diego County, California, hereby make and declare this to be my last Will, and revoke all other Wills and Codicils previously made by me.

I

I declare that I am now unmarried. I have one child now living, an adult, namely: KEITH MAILLARD.

II

I give, devise and bequeath all of my estate, of whatever character
and kind, and wherever situated, in equal shares, share and share
alike, to the following two (2) Masonic charities, namely: (a) to
the KNIGHTS TEMPLAR EYE FOUNDATION, INC., a
nonprofit corporation, located in Springfield, Illinois; and (b) to
the SHRINERS HOSPITAL FOR CRIPPLED CHILDREN, a
Colorado nonprofit corporation, located in Tampa, Florida.

III

I have intentionally omitted to provide in this Will for my son
KEITH MAILLARD. Under no circumstances is he, or any
of his issue, to ever receive a part of my estate. . . . My executor
is hereby authorized to defend, at the expense of my estate, any
contest or other attack of any nature on this will or any of its
provisions.

I felt as though I'd been kicked in the balls. The will seemed
actively malevolent to me. There was nothing vague about it,
nothing that might suggest another interpretation—I'd been
singled out by name and denied. I'd known that I wasn't a
beneficiary, but the words in the will hit me like a "fuck you" from
the grave.

It was as though I'd suffered a wound so old I'd forgotten all
about it, but one that had never quite healed, and now it was laid
open again, slashed with either of those damned knives that had
already turned up in this narrative. If you learn nothing else in
therapy, you learn that you can't help what you're feeling, so I was

stuck feeling it, suffering through it again, and I hated what it was doing to me. I was not a calm, mature, middle-aged man who found things *interesting*. I was as angry as Jehovah, raging at my dead father from the blazing mile-high tower of my self-righteous fury: "What did I do to deserve *this*? What did I ever *do* to you? *You hurt me, you son of a bitch.*"

"If he'd left me a gold pocket watch," I told Mary, "If he'd left me a ring, if he'd left me a goddamned letter . . ."

That's it, I thought, a letter was exactly what I'd wanted— maybe my secret wish. I'd wanted to open the envelope and find a letter. It didn't have to be a long letter, any letter would do—"Dear Keith, I have thought of you over these years . . ."

Some gesture, some acknowledgment that I was his son, a piece of his life, something from his heart, something personal, *anything*, but, no, it was exactly the way it had always been. Nothing. How could he have done that? It wasn't that he hadn't known a thing about me. He'd known that I was a writer in Canada. Surely he could have found something to say to me. "Dear Keith, as you know, your mother and I didn't get along, but I've always regretted . . ."

I was still carrying Gene's glasses around in my bag. I'm not an impulsive person, but as I was walking across campus the next morning, I grabbed them out of my bag, threw them onto the pavement and stomped on them. Plastic lenses, unfortunately, do not shatter. They do pop out of the frames. I ground them under my heel. I twisted the frames into an unidentifiable tangle of wire and threw them into the garbage can. It didn't help.

Okay, I thought, I can get my own damned lawyer. I called one in California. "The language is boilerplate," he said. "In order to make a large bequest to a charity stick, the heirs have to be specifically disinherited. Don't take it personally."

Don't take it personally? *Under no circumstances is he, or any of his issue, to ever receive a part of my estate . . .* My *issue*—that is, Gene's seven-year-old granddaughter who was proudly telling the other kids "My grandfather was a tap dancer."

The will had pretty well nailed things down, but there was one way we could attack it, the lawyer said. Because Gene had been so active in the Masons, had already donated so much to the Masons, because his executor had been a Mason and his lawyer a Mason, we could argue that the Masons had exerted "undue influence" over him. It was far from a slam-dunk. Chances were good that we wouldn't win it, but the named Masonic charities might part with some of the money just to stop the suit because we could tie them up in probate for years. Did I want to do that?

I had to think about it. "The thing you've got to remember," I told Mary, "is that when I was little, there were no men in my life. Not just no *occasional* men, I mean no men, period. I knew what they were, that they *existed*. But I didn't like them. I was afraid of them. I don't know when I realized that I had a father . . . that I *didn't* have a father."

I paced up and down our bedroom, trying to talk through it with my wife—going on and on because I couldn't find the end of the thread. "If I tried to break his goddamn will," I said, "it'd be sheer retaliation. I don't give a shit about his money."

"You have to write your way through this," she said.

That stopped me. I couldn't do that. Write about what? How?

Trying to read my father into my life, I'd been forced to read the absence of something rather than the presence of something. I'd tried to read the blackness of the shadow—to read what wasn't there—because nothing was there. I'd thought that all other kids had fathers but I didn't. I felt that it was shameful not to have a father, so I wouldn't talk about it, not ever. Gene

Maillard had refused to exist for me, so I'd tried to will him into nonexistence.

I invented any number of fictional fathers for myself, but I didn't know that's what they were. Around the time I was eight, I became passionately interested in fishing. I bought fishing magazines, read books on fishing from the library, sent away in the mail for more books, and gradually assembled in my mind the image of a man who went fishing. He came partially from *Field and Stream*, partially from ordinary men I would have seen around me—that was, after all, West Virginia—a rumpled fellow, gruff but kind, a grown man who smoked a pipe and wore baggy khaki-colored pants, work boots, plaid flannel shirts, an old ripped baggy jacket, and a slouch hat with fishing flies stuck into it. I didn't burden him with a family or a job; he went out and caught fish, and that was all he did. He was *the fisherman*.

I became obsessed and began to collect rods and reels and lures and sundry other gear. I learned about the three different kinds of rods—bait-casting, fly-casting, and spinning. I saved my allowances and my birthday money because I knew I would need all three. I bought the reels to go with them and the proper filament of fishing line. I began collecting lures and bought myself a tackle box to store them in. My favorite lure was a medium-sized one for bass. It had little metal wings on it to make it roll in the water. It was supposed to look so much like an injured fish that a bigger fish would strike immediately.

Then I became obsessed with trout fishing because you could buy brilliantly colored flies with wonderful names like "royal coachman." I bought a fly-tying kit with vices that clamped to the edge of my desk and a big bright mirror so I could see the back of the fly while I was working on it. I bought floss and peacock hurl and thread and everything else I needed and I tied all the traditional patterns. I made a perfect set of royal coachmen, filed off the points on the hooks, mounted them to earring clips, and gave them to my mother for her birthday. She said she liked them, but she never wore them.

I tied dozens of flies and collected more and more lures and gradually accumulated everything I could possibly need. I knew all about the various kinds of bait—all the way from the dough balls and worms you'd use to catch catfish in the Ohio River to the various lures for trolling and, of course, the beautiful flies for trout fishing. I knew that I was going to have to think like a trout, pick the fly that looked like the insects on the water that day, and put it where the trout had just risen in the stream. Or, if I was on a boat, I could go trolling for bass. I was all set with my spinning reel too. I knew I'd be able to cast much farther with it because of the way the line came off the reel. So I knew all about fishing, and I was ready. The only thing missing was *the fisherman*, that grown man in his rumpled jacket and his flannel shirt, smoking his pipe, who would take me fishing and show me how to do it and keep me company. I collected all this gear and all these lures and tied all these flies, and I never once went fishing, and I never once caught a single fish.

"You never told me that story," my wife said.

I don't think through the major decisions in my life. The "click"— that moment when I know what I'm going to do—almost always happens in my sleep. A few days after I'd received Gene's will, I woke up and I was clear about it.

I'd always wanted a direct communication from my father, and I'd got one. No one could convince me that it was not personal. The words in his will might have been legal boilerplate, but he had signed his name to them. My father had lived to be nearly ninety-six years old. In all of that time, he had sent me only one message, and this was it:

Keith,

I know that you are living and that you are an adult. Neither you nor your children will ever get a thing from me. I would rather that all of my money went to my lawyer than for you to get a penny of it.

Now that I'd had a chance to absorb the shock, I understood that I had not been the main thing on his mind. He'd wanted to make sure that his money would go where he'd wanted it to go, and he'd probably seen me as little more than an inconvenience, but, insofar as he'd thought about me at all, he'd decided to hurt me, and he'd succeeded. If I tried to match my father's hostility with my own, it would be—as sappy as it might sound—bad karma. I was not going to try to break his will. Some money would be nice, there was no denying it, but I really didn't care about his money.

I called my mother. She was eighty-six, still living on her own in West Virginia. "Well, Gene died," I said. "I heard it from his lawyer."

"Oh? Did he leave you anything?"

"No."

I listened to her silence until she found what she wanted to say. "I'm glad I outlived him."

I had always suspected that my parents hated each other, but I wasn't quite ready to hear that brutal line of my mother's—the bleak satisfaction in her flat delivery. It chilled me. What could have happened between them terrible enough to get them to that point? Whatever it was, it had happened in Hot Springs, Arkansas. In order to understand my parents, I'd have to understand Hot Springs, but it was just another black hole—and why should I bother trying to understand anything? Why should I care about Eugene Charles Maillard, that *unusual* man? Once again he did not feel like my father. I felt what I'd always felt—that I didn't have a father.

4.

FRAPPÉ PAR UNE VOITURE

M. Louis Maillard Est Victime D'un Accident Fatal.

I DON'T KNOW ANY FRENCH AT ALL, but I didn't need any to translate the headline—"Monsieur Louis Maillard Is a Victim of a Fatal Accident." Mary, like most other Canadians, had years of French in school, never learned enough to be able to carry on a conversation, but still has a fuzzy useful cloud of the language floating around in her head. "What's *frappé*?" I said.

"Struck," she said. "He was struck by a runaway carriage."

"That's Gene's grandfather," Gus Klammer told us.

Gene's grandfather was *my great-grandfather*. I stared at his picture in the yellowed newspaper clipping—an old bald guy with a flat head and a white moustache. Once again, this was too much too fast. Just as when my father's lawyer had first called me, I was feeling—to use that brainless but useful word—stunned. Mary asked the question for both of us: "Did he tell you anything about him?"

"He probably did," Gus said, "but I don't remember. Gene talked a lot about what's in those scrapbooks. He was always worrying about them. 'Gus, you make sure the scrapbooks are safe.'"

Given Gene's animus toward me, he probably wouldn't have been pleased to know that I had his precious scrapbooks, but I did have them nonetheless, and I was delighted to have them. I already knew that they were a gold mine for me, more valuable than any amount of money. I was still trying to absorb the impact of opening the black scrapbook and seeing a newspaper clipping *in French*. It was one thing to have always known that I was French—as a story—but quite another to see the proof of it. There was the French connection, the *Canadian* connection, documented on the first page. I felt vindicated. The family legend was *true*. That meant that I must surely have cousins in Quebec somewhere, speaking French. Maybe I could even find them.

"Did you know he spoke French?" I asked Gus. That was another thing my mother had always told me.

"I knew he spoke it, but I never heard him speak it."

"How did he pronounce his name?" Mary asked.

"That's funny," Gus said. "He pronounced it 'My-yard.' If somebody asked him, he'd always say, '*your* yard . . . *my* yard.' After that, you never forgot it."

Mary was working her way through the French in the newspaper clipping. "Damn. There's no date on it. You'd think your father would have put a date on it . . . Anyhow, an ambulance was . . . dispatched . . . to transport the body of a man who'd been the victim of a fatal accident. It's even got his address." She pointed it out to me: *"M. Louis Maillard, bourgeois, âgé de 62 ans et demeurant au No 1032 Rue Sainte-Catherine Est . . ."*

"In Montreal?"

"Right. *Le défunt était bièn connu à Montréal.* He was . . . I guess walking northeast at the corners of Dorion and Sainte-Catherine Streets when he was struck by the carriage going west. He was . . ."

I could even translate the next part, or at least some of it—*Il fut violentment projeté sur la chaussée, et dans sa chute se fractura le crâne*—"Thrown violently . . . his skull fractured."

"And the ambulance arrived immediately, but . . . *avant que des soins puissent lui etre donnnés* . . . I guess they did their best. But the victim has already expired . . . Oh, and . . . What's *pénible*? It's like sad . . . or, I don't know, sadly ironic . . ."

"Pathetic?" I said. "Pitiable? Lamentable? . . . What are we doing? Making up French?"

"*Détail particulièrement pénible* . . . He was killed *sous les yeux de son épouse* . . . right in front of his wife. She was on the other side of the street."

"Oh. That's fairly horrible."

"Look at this. He was a French veteran . . . 1870, 1871. What war was going on then?"

"The War of the Roses?"

"Oh, come on, Keith. Maybe the Franco-Prussian. Anyhow, the Veterans' organization assisted at his funeral. It doesn't list the surviving family members, but I bet we've got enough information to find him."

Gus Klammer, my father's executor, had turned out to be just as upbeat in person as he'd sounded on the phone—a walking testimony to Masonic optimism. He'd brought us the scrapbooks on his way to a Shriners' convention on Vancouver Island—"a bunch of old guys like me," he said. "We're going to swap yarns and drink so much we'll all be sorry." He was in his late eighties, with clear blue eyes and a full head of white and pewter hair. He wore a hearing aid but radiated a strong vigorous animal health. In all the pictures I have of him, he regards the camera with a gravely composed face as though he considered each photograph to be a serious ritual, but in my memory, he's always grinning. "I used to live around here," he said.

"No!" Mary said, "you're kidding."

"Yeah, about a block from here." Our part of West Vancouver had been cottage country in the late 30s when the Lions Gate Bridge had just been built. Gus remembered the corner store up the street from us on Marine Drive. I'd forgotten that Gus was originally a Canadian. "Small world," Gus and Mary were saying to each other, "what a coincidence."

Gus had also brought my father's last pair of tap shoes— ordinary men's loafers with the taps screwed onto them. They were pink. Gus told us that Gene was so cheap that he never considered buying new tap shoes; whatever show he was in during his last years, he just painted those old loafers to match his costume. There was no possibility of my following, literally, in my father's footsteps. Like me, he had small feet, but his were much narrower than mine, and I couldn't get his tap shoes on.

Gus had a cup of tea with us and then went on his way—the last thing he said to me, shaking his head sadly: "You were so *easy* to find."

Gene had filled two scrapbooks—a black one and a brown one. His business card was pasted onto each: "Entertainer Gene Maillard—Singer, Writer/Composer, Marimba Player, Tap Dancer, Monologist." Our first impression was one of total chaos— oh, my God, it would take us years to understand all the material Gene had collected. There were pictures to be studied, clippings to be read, objects that needed to be handled and opened—a dizzying kaleidoscope of images ranging from small fading black-and-white photographs to the brilliantly colored covers of playbills. Everything was mounted on a thick, coarse paper that had dried and gone brown over the years; whenever we turned a page, bits of it crumbled away. Some of the newspaper clippings were well preserved, but others had yellowed, cracked, and lost parts of their text. Just by looking at the scrapbooks, we were destroying them, but we had to know what was in them.

It wasn't until we had been through them several times that we began to see that Gene had arranged his artifacts in roughly chronological order. Just as he'd told Gus, he'd documented most of his life, beginning with the death of his grandfather, then moving on through his childhood and into his early manhood— Gene with his first car, Gene in a football uniform, Gene playing drums in a 20s dance band—to arrive at a trim middle-aged man with lines around his eyes and a natty hairline moustache. There were dozens of pictures of Gene and his students dancing. When he'd reached 1950, he'd run out of pages in the black scrapbook, so he'd continued in the brown.

The brown scrapbook was far less interesting. Gene retired in 1964. He preserved his memories of a vacation in Florida with Kodacolor snapshots, of a cruise in the South Pacific with ship's menus. A large section was devoted to Kippy and her career, beginning with her as a cute kid tap-dancing on roller skates and ending with her as a professional entertainer playing her harp at the Dunes. The last documents in the brown scrapbook are cancelled checks that Gene had written to several Masonic organizations when he was in his eighties.

The black scrapbook was the one that counted. It covered the first fifty years of Gene's life and had to be crammed with clues to everything I'd ever wanted to know about my father. The first thing pasted there was the French clipping—"*Frappé Par Une Voiture*"—and then, as we turned the pages, we found old family photographs, primarily of Gene. A formal shot of his grade school class with Gene sitting in the first row. A studio portrait of him as a one-year-old in a white dress, standing upright and supporting himself on a wickerwork chair. Another, taken a year or so later, in a pinstripe tunic with knickers and a broad military belt.

The photograph that kept drawing us back to it was one that had been pasted onto the first page along with the clipping about Louis Maillard's death. Gene, as a child of about eight, is standing with a woman who appears to be in her sixties and a man with a moustache who appears to be in his late thirties. Both Gene and the man are wearing dark trousers and white dress shirts, but the man is also wearing a vest and a bow tie. A straw hat, the kind called a "boater," is tilted back on his forehead, a bit of hairline visible under it. He's squinting slightly. His eyes are like Gene's—the small, baggy, allergic eyes that seem to have characterized my father his whole life—the same eyes that both Liz and I have. One of the man's hands is resting lightly on Gene's shoulder. Looking through a magnifying glass, we could see that the man hasn't bothered to remove a small pipe from his mouth.

The older woman stands to Gene's left, directly behind him. She's a short, heavy, small-boned woman with a flattened, squared-off face, wearing a long dark striped dress, her hair severely up in a bun. Like Gene and the man, she has small eyes, but she doesn't have those distinctive allergic pouches under them. The three of them are regarding the camera with somber faces—the photograph is awash in sadness. "It must be Louis's funeral," Mary said. "Gene with his father and grandmother." If she was right, then Louis must have died in 1909.

I'm not sure that I ever managed to convey to Mary the full enormity of what I was feeling. *It's true,* I kept thinking, *it's all true.* Gene really did speak French. His family really did live in

Canada. These were not people in my childhood fantasy; these were real people.

When I was nine, my mother and I went to visit my uncle Addison in Buffalo—he'd moved there to work for Eastman Kodak—and it was the farthest away from Wheeling I'd ever been. I loved the train ride, the animals in the Buffalo Zoo, and seeing my favorite uncle again. I was at exactly the right age for Niagara Falls, felt that mind-altering blow-out of transcendence that the natural world can sometimes give us—the roar of it, the sheer magnificent size of that avalanche of water, especially at night with colored floodlights shining on it. A million tourists blasted off their flashbulbs trying to capture the Falls—which made Addison, the professional photographer, laugh. "That's like firing pea-shooters at an elephant." He took us to a place where they lent us raincoats, and we got to walk *behind* the falls. I could reach out and touch the water—Neato! But the best thing about the trip was going to Canada.

It was *a foreign country*—that made it a big deal. I experienced the border crossing with religious awe. We were *leaving the United States*, we were *entering another country*. I felt as alive and twitchy as a crawfish. Addison had told me that I shouldn't do anything to make the border guard mad; if he got mad, he might not let us in. The guard asked Addison and my mother where they were born. Addison said Chicago, and my mother said Pittsburgh, and I yelled out from the back seat, "I was born in Wheeling, West Virginia." My mother shushed me, but the man said, "Thank you."

I had a secret I kept to myself—I felt it swelling up inside me like a little radiant egg—Addison and my mother were visitors there, *foreigners*, but I wasn't. This was my father's country, and because half of me had come from him, it was my country too. I belonged in that foreign country in a way that they didn't.

I wanted everything to be immediately different. I wanted the people, the buildings, the trees, *the grass* to be different and was disappointed when they weren't. I wanted everyone to be speaking French. My mother told me that we weren't in the part of Canada where they spoke French. She told me that the King of England was the King of Canada too—that's why his picture was on the money—and she bought some Canadian money for me so that I could take it home with me and keep it forever. I got some postcards too—with the Falls and Mounties on them—and a little Canadian flag. The Maple Leaf hadn't been created yet, so it was the old Red Ensign, and it had its own little silver flag pole.

When we came home, I pinned my Canadian flag up on my wall and asked my mother to send away mail-order for language records so I could learn French. My mother had named me Keith because I deserved my own name, but there had always been, quite clearly in my mind, that other boy I might have been, the one who'd been named after his father. Now he came vividly alive for me. I imagined him like the drawings in the booklets that came with the Linguaphone records. Eugene Maillard the Fourth wore shorts and a beret, carried a basket with a wine bottle and a long skinny loaf of bread sticking out of it, spoke French, and lived in Canada with other Maillards who had brown eyes and spoke French.

If you're a child in Wheeling, West Virginia, in 1951, it's going to take more than Linguaphone to teach you French. I approached the language with awe—wouldn't allow myself to go on to the next step until I was certain that I could do the first one perfectly—but with nobody to help me, I could never be *absolutely certain* I was right. I repeated the first few bands on the first record over and over. French was my father's language, and that made it just too damned important, so, to this day, I can't speak a word of it. I never got beyond Linguaphone Lesson Number One: *"Le Français est la langue universelle."*

5.

IN THE SCRAPBOOKS, GENE HAD SAVED two newspaper articles about his life in show business. On Saturday, February 2, 1963, the *Columbia Basin News* had run the headline—"Busy Years But Pleasant Ones, 'Music Man' Reminisces." A photograph shows Gene with one of his students, a little girl of about six, wearing shorts and tap shoes. He's sitting on a bench behind her, holding each of her hands in his as she smiles at the camera. The interview opens by telling us that "Gene Maillard . . . quite literally has more 'bounce to the ounce' than most youngsters one-fourth his age."

> Though now eligible for retirement from his job in the construction engineering department of General Electric Co., this slender song and dance man, music composer, choreographer, show director, master of ceremonies and a host of other talented facets, just doesn't pictorially fit into any senior-age bracket.
>
> His dancing feet have tapped their way through almost every day of his life since he was a youngster. Born in Pennsylvania, Gene comes quite honestly by his love for rhythm of all kinds. His French paternal grandfather played tuba and directed military bands in Montréal, Canada, as well as doing some composing. Twin aunts played pianos and two half-brothers became professional musicians in separate bands.

"Mostly because they couldn't get along very well," the Tri-Cities man explains this division of brothers' journeys through orchestra and band years. While the other family members were tooting trumpets or trombones, Gene was teaching himself dance routines until he was 17 years old.

Mary had already started a file on Gene's grandfather, Louis Maillard. Now she could add "musician" to it. She opened new files on "twin aunts who played piano" and "half-brothers in bands." I wasn't as optimistic as she was that we would ever find anything to add to those files.

Gene, I read, "was apt to break into a lively demonstration of how American tap dancing was evolved from the good old Irish jig." It pleased the professor in me that my father had known about the origins of his art and had been able to demonstrate it.

Maillard started teaching dancing in 1924 and when he went to New York and the Bronx, found himself with an ideal setup for meeting people, making friends and going places, through answering an ad in the paper for a dance instructor.

"The woman who placed the ad needed someone for teaching evenings and told me, "No salary but everything you take in is yours," Gene recalled. "I never had it so good." His price was 25 cents a lesson for three hours.

Contacts in New York kept him in touch with the world behind the footlights and in 1927, Gene was playing roles with stock companies in the Colonial Theatre of Cleveland. . . .

Fortune carried Maillard into West Virginia and there he starred on the weekly Mutual radio broadcast of the Wheeling Steel Hour. . . . The then-young male singer and dancer, who by this time was writing melodies and lyrics for his dance patterns—eventually with 38 copyrights of his own—became producer of the annual Wheeling Steel Show, put on by the company with its own talent.

This included male choruses, black-face-routine minstrel selections, ballads and dancing, all directed and with choreography by this young man whose very thoughts were in rhythm. Oh, yes, and the stage settings—not only were these designed but also engineered by Maillard whose education in drafting assisted his plans.

During the 1930s, all big Eastern companies seemed to delight in producing big shows. "While I was working with the Sanderson & Porter Construction Company, once a year they'd give me leave to work up a big review for them. Those were a busy five years, but you can imagine what pleasant ones," the Kennewick "dance" man said.

Occasions awakening his songwriting abilities have been many and unique. Like the one he wrote about his troubles with pesky mosquitoes during his stay in Louisiana; a catchy tune and words written for favorite nephew Jimmy, while the uncle was riding from one town to another by car; a song mostly for Christmas Eve, set to the words of the classic poem for tots, "Twas the Night Before Christmas" and a wedding present melody for another nephew and his bride.

Maillard has a letter from the Bureau of patents showing his copyright claims for a song "Bouncy," filed one month and four days before the filing for Irving Berlin's now famous "Got the Sun in the Morning" from "Annie, Get Your Gun." Lyrics, of course, don't match, but the melody is virtually the same, note for note.

"Though I was hardly in a position to fight such a name as Irving Berlin, it gave me a lot of pleasure to know I was writing songs along the same line," the composer said as he folded the script of the song and returned it to his file.

During his Tri-City's residence years, Maillard, in 1948, put on and directed an entire show in the Atomic City entitled "Our Richland," for which he wrote songs as well. He puts on shows and entertainments for such groups as the Elks, Masonic lodges and the El Katif Shrine Club and Patrol. He is a wide-awake drummer for the latter group and if those men parade especially lively in some performance, you can be sure that beat originates under those hands to whom music has been a way of life.

Philosophy for genial Gene, the "Music Man" of this vicinity, is summed up thus, "Dancing has always made me friends and opened many doors, that's why I've never given it up."

Twelve years later, Gene told his life story again, this time in the *Times-Advocate* in Escondido, California, Friday, June 20, 1975—"74-Year-Old Hoofer Uses Skill to Keep Trim." The accompanying photograph shows Gene brushing the taps on his tap shoes—the very same shoes, painted pink, that were now resting by my fireplace.

Years of tap dancing have paid off for Eugene Maillard of Escondido.

Billed as a "young 74-year-old," he has maintained a trim appearance by dancing since his childhood. He has used his skill to pay his way through college, to earn an extra salary, to entertain others and to relax himself.

His talent was recognized here this spring when he placed second in the senior citizens talent contest for all of San Diego County.

Maillard began to dance while just a tot in Pennsylvania. His older brothers organized a band, and young Gene kicked up his heels when they played.

"I turned out to be a ham," he said. "I just got up and performed."

He studied for the Ministry for two and a half years at Bethany College in Bethany, West Virginia, but was disappointed by the behavior of some classmates and decided to enter another field.

Maillard paid for two years of studies at Carnegie Institute of Technology in Pittsburgh by teaching tap dancing as an elective course. He recommended the class to give coordination and timing to athletes and drama students. He also gave dancing exhibitions and poetry recitations at various colleges and groups.

"Back in those days tap dancing was all the rage," he recalled. He has seen tap dancing go through three cycles of popularity, and he expects it to be acclaimed again soon.

Maillard worked for 42 years as a draftsman and designer, advancing to the position of senior designer for General Electric at a nuclear reactor in Hanford, Washington. During his free time in those years, he taught tap dancing and entertained wherever his work took him.

He moonlighted in theaters and summer stock productions and staged shows for the various firms employing him. Maillard even organized a variety review, "Gene Maillard and His Gum Band," which squeezed 33 acts into an hour-long presentation.

A thick scrapbook bulging with clippings testifies to his numerous performances.

Now a member of the Harmonaires band at the Joslyn Senior Center in Escondido, Maillard took up the trombone when his doctor advised blowing exercises to combat a chronic lung ailment.

"I'd rather blow into something that makes music," he said. He also plays the guitar and marimbas, and he writes music as well.

Maillard still rises at 7 each morning to dance a half hour both before and after breakfast, then to practice on the trombone and marimbas. He has made many appearances at the senior center, including a starring role in the "Love Story in song" show for the center's first anniversary.

"I've always used my music and tap dancing as an outlet," he said.

6.

IN GENE'S PERSONAL EFFECTS I'd found a card with an address and phone number for a Doctor Frank Wade in Williamsport, Pennsylvania. The moment I'd seen the name, I'd known that I'd heard it before. I called the number; the man who answered said that, yes, he was Frank Wade. I told him that I was Gene Maillard's son.

He seemed delighted to hear from me. "Of course I know who you are. I held you on my lap when you were a baby."

"You did?"

"Your mother was a tall, dark-haired woman?"

"Um," I said. That wasn't a good start. My mother was short and blond. I asked him how he and I were related.

He laughed. "Well, that's kind of hard to explain. Our family's kind of mixed up. It's like the United Nations. The simplest way to put it? You and I share the same grandmother."

Our grandmother, Clementine, had been married three times. First to a man named Tommasini, then to Frank's grandfather, a man named Serpagli, and then to a man named Maillard. "Do you remember my grandfather?" I asked.

"No, he was dead before I was born."

But he did remember my father—vividly. Frank's mother,

Olga Serpagli, was Gene's older half-sister. That would make Frank my half-first-cousin. "I can never remember not knowing Uncle Gene," Frank said. "Yeah, I always knew him, right from the time I was a baby. He would live with us for a while, then he'd move out, maybe go somewhere else on a job, and then he'd come back again."

Gene used to sit in their kitchen with a hair-growing machine on his head. Frank didn't remember much more about it than that—it was supposed to make your hair grow, and it had a gadget like a cap that moved up and down and massaged your head. Gene had started to lose his hair young, and he was very sensitive about it.

"He smoked a long cherry wood pipe," Frank said. "It seemed *very* long. He'd sit there with this thing going up and down, up and down, and he'd smoke that pipe. Funny as hell, but you didn't dare laugh. He'd kill you, if you laughed at him. You'd put your hand over your mouth and chuckle inwardly. Wooden stem and a wooden bowl, maybe a little clay lining inside it. I don't ever recall him smoking cigarettes, and he didn't smoke that pipe often. When he did, it was mostly when he was sitting under this hair-growing thing. He'd sit there with his pipe in his hand. He looked really like he was almost meditating."

Gene, Frank told me, had gone to Bethany College, but he'd been expelled for participating in that ancient collegiate prank of putting a cow up the belfry. For a while, he'd rented the second floor of an old bank building in Wellsburg, West Virginia, and taught tap there.

I asked him about the grandmother we had in common. He remembered her as a very short woman with her hair pulled tight into a bun at the back. She spoke French and a number of dialects of Italian and worked as an interpreter for the City of Pittsburgh.

The family legend had it that when she'd been a little girl in a convent school near Paris, her two older brothers had kidnapped her and brought her to America.

"Well," I said, "if her name was Mariani and she came from Parma, she must have been Italian."

"Oh, no," Frank said. "Grandmother Maillard always told me that she was French."

Talking to Frank Wade sent me back to the black scrapbook to study facing pages near the end. Each featured a young woman. On the left-hand page was a yellowed, undated newspaper clipping, crumbling at the edges, starring a blonde named Mademoiselle Ruth Maillard.

> Being a young woman who has been around no end, the idea of getting about the world—in other words traveling—has no special sensation to Ruth Maillard, chorus girl in the line at Nick Albenese "Arabian Gardens." Mlle. Maillard believes that any town, even Columbus, can afford all the novelty that one might find in a tour of European capitals. So closely followed by a Sunday Star photographer she sets out on a sort of Fry-cook's tour.

There are five newspaper photographs of Mlle. Maillard. In one, she is standing with one hand on the edge of a stone balustrade looking out over the skyline of Columbus, Ohio, which she finds "just as good as the Parisian product." In other pictures, she is eating spaghetti in the Southern Hotel, looking at postcards at a newsstand, lying in a bathtub with a little boat floating next to her. In the largest of the pictures, Mlle. Maillard is relaxing in her hotel room—a sign next to her says, "Do Not Disturb"—lying back in a chair with a drink in one hand and a cigarette in the other, her feet propped up on a chair, her skirt hiked up to show off her platform heels and her long, lovely showgirl's legs. She's a Jean Harlow blonde with exactly the kind of figure you would expect a showgirl to have. Onto this clipping, Gene has pasted another clipping.

> Arabian Gardens Deluxe Night Club, Sunday and Monday nights only, Duke Ellington and his Famous Orchestra with Ivie Anderson, returned by your insistent demand.

The young lady on the page opposite to Mlle. Maillard couldn't have been more different—a dewy-fresh girl no older than twenty, a brunette with huge luminous dark eyes and a gardenia in her curly bobbed hair. There's no date on the newspaper clipping, but Gene has written 1924.

ENGAGEMENT TO LOCAL MAN IS ANNOUNCED BY MOTHER

> Miss Cochrane's engagement to E. C. Maillard of Pittsburgh has been announced by her mother, Mrs. W. G. Cochrane, formerly of Dormont Avenue, Dormont. No date has been set for the wedding. Miss Cochrane, who was a popular member of the Dormont younger set, will give a house party next week in the Cochrane's new home in Cleveland where they moved last week. A number of her Pittsburgh friends will be guests.

I was sure that Mlle. Ruth Maillard and Lynette Rose Cochrane were Gene's first two wives. "Doesn't it seem odd to you," I said to Mary, "that he would have kept souvenirs of Ruth and Lynette and none of my mother?"

"No," she said, "it doesn't seem the least bit odd. Your mother was the one that really hurt."

My half-cousin, Frank Wade, had invited me to call him again, so I did. "That baby you saw . . . It couldn't have been me. I was born in 1942."

"Yeah, you' re right," he said. "I've been thinking about it too. I was just a kid in 1930, so it couldn't have been you. I thought that baby was Gene's son, but I've probably got it confused with something else. But I know I met Gene's wife. I remember her clearly. She was a tall, slender, dark-haired, good-looking woman. Classy. She was very nice to me, very kind to me. She was not a particularly loquacious individual . . . I think I saw her maybe two or three times at the most . . . Your dad was popular with women. He had a lot of women friends, but marriages just didn't succeed with him. I don't know why."

Since our first phone call, Frank had been thinking about more than the baby on his lap. When Gene had been in his eighties, he had hopped a Greyhound bus and ridden it all the way from Escondido to Williamsport to visit Frank and his wife Joy. He'd told Frank that he was planning to leave his estate, or at least a part of it, to the Wades. "I don't care about your estate, Gene," Frank had told him. "Leave something to us if you want. I'm just glad you're here."

A few years after that Gene stopped writing to them, and they didn't know why. "When he was dying, nobody bothered to call and tell us. After Gene's funeral was over, I got a call from Gene's executor, that Gus Klammer character. Seems that Gene had left all his money to the Masons. He'd never said a word to me about leaving his money to the Masons."

Frank asked if I had considered trying to break Gene's will. I said I'd considered it and told him about talking to the lawyer. "Maybe you should have done it," he said. "I think you would have had a pretty good case."

"Maybe," I said. I didn't want to explain my idea of bad karma, so I hurried the conversation along in other directions. I told him that Gene had talked in his newspaper interviews about two older half-brothers who played in bands.

"Probably would have been John and Louis," he said, "but I didn't know that either one of them played instruments. They may have. They were the only half-brothers I know, unless . . . See, I told you there were three different fathers. Except for Uncle Frank Serpagli and my mother, no two of them had the same set of parents. So Uncle John and Uncle Louis would have been two half-brothers."

I told him that Gene had said he was studying for the ministry at Bethany. Frank laughed outright at that.

Gene? Study for ministry? That's really funny. That's ridiculous . . . The way I remember it, several boys had been involved in that stunt with the cow, but Gene was the only one who owned up to it, so he was the only one who got expelled. He never forgave the other guys for not coming forward.

I always thought about Gene . . . Well, he always had a lot of unusual things about him. I remember I was in a play in high school, and I was the villain. Gene had this artificial flower that you put in your buttonhole, and it had a tube and a bulb down in your pocket, and I filled that sucker up with water, and when the hero went to get by me on the stage, he got a squirt right in the eye! He didn't know what the hell happened. Gene was sitting right in the front row, and he knew what I'd done. He laughed his head off. He said, "I should have stopped you from doing that," and I said, "Well, it didn't hurt anything," and he said, "No, it just made the show better."

He had all kinds of things like that, little gadgets all over the place. Like that theatrical make-up case. It's hard to describe his versatility. Truly. I've always thought that in other days he probably would have . . . Not that he wasn't successful, in his later life. But it was the Depression. He could have been far more successful. He was very talented, but his talents weren't limited to one thing. You know, he was inventive.

7.

SO WHAT WAS I SUPPOSED TO DO with this avalanche of new information about my *inventive* father? Was I supposed to write something about him? I was still too pissed off at him to do that. Everything I was learning about him suggested that he might have been a good father for me—if he'd been around—but he *hadn't* been around. The person who *had* been around was Mrs. Mabel Sharp.

My grandmother was the stable center of my childhood. She rests at the bottom of my psyche like a rock. You could agree with her, or disagree with her, but you never had to wonder what she was thinking. One of her standard lines was, "It's a great life if you don't weaken." She categorized people clearly and firmly. She never hesitated, and once people were categorized, they stayed that way. She'd grown up in a fiercely Unionist town where folks had still been talking about the Civil War, so she had no use for southerners—a prejudice she passed on to my mother. The Lebanese people who lived in the apartment building with us were "the hunkies upstairs." Germans had been in the Valley for almost as long as we had, so our other upstairs neighbors were not hunkies, and my grandmother had no special name for them, but she made it clear that they were different from us. She never used "hillbilly" as a term of opprobrium. Hillbillies were people who lived, just as

57

their name suggested, off in the hills; they were rural, uneducated, and famously amusing, but there wasn't anything irremediably wrong with them. There was a big strange clotted family a few streets over from us, migrants from someplace "downstate," which is what we called anything south of Cameron. "Everybody sleeps with everybody," people said about them, and I imagined them in a huge bed that took up an entire room, the whole lot of them sprawled around on it, snoring away. My grandmother did not call those people "hillbillies," and she did not call them "trash" either—that was not a term she ever used. They were simply "no good." If people were no good, they were tainted all the way down to their bone marrow. There was no hope for them, and nothing they could do would ever change their category.

Men were clearly seen as the rulers of the universe, but, at the same time, they were not to be trusted. Men could be no good, but, more often, they were merely weak. Ray, the local pharmacist, lived in our building. He was a binge drinker and sometimes got so plastered he passed out in the hallway; I remember once having to step over him to get to our apartment. But he was from a good family, worked for a living, owned his own business, and when he was sober, "you'd never know a nicer guy"—so you couldn't call him no good. He was weak, and that was understandable, even to some extent forgivable. My uncle Bill was another man who was weak. My grandmother was downtown shopping once and ran into a friend who said to her, meaning it as a compliment, "No matter how drunk he gets, Bill is always a gentleman." My grandmother was mortified, but she was also secretly satisfied, because it indicated that Bill, however weak he was, had not yet sunk to the level of being no good. My grandmother's exiled husband had clearly been weak. I don't know how my father would have been characterized because no one ever talked about him.

On rare occasions you might run across a strong man. There

were a few of those in my childhood—like my grandmother's beloved father, Everett Thomas, the riverboat captain who did what a man should do, worked on the river, provided for his family, and never weakened. Among the living relatives, there were a few strong men like my uncle Addison, but not many. Most of the men you'd ordinarily meet were not strong at all; they were shifty, shady, difficult fellows you had to baby, the way my grandmother babied my uncle Bill. Men like that had to be looked after by mature women who had common sense and never weakened. Far too often, men could go sideways on you, run around and refuse to work. They could take to the bottle, or take to the cards or, in the case of my father, simply take off.

If I were writing myself as a character in a novel, I would long ago have taken some pains to place myself in the times, but children don't see the times as *the times*, and when I try to connect what I remember from childhood with the state of the nation, all I can produce are a few odd fragments. Before I could even begin to understand what a war was, ours was over and we'd won it. As a small child, I loved going to the movies; some of the things I watched were newsreels, but to me, they were all just movies. I liked watching things blow up, and on the screens of the Court and the Capitol and the Liberty Theaters, things blew up a lot. I had no reason to be afraid of the atomic bomb. I liked its mushroom cloud and low rumble. It was the biggest bomb there was, but it was *our* bomb. It would be years before I would understand what it had done to people.

Harry S. Truman was the president of the United States and had been as long as I could remember. Even now, if I heard his voice, I'd know it, because I heard him on the radio and will never forget him, not anything he said, but *the sound of his voice*—the voice of the man who ran the country.

We liked Harry okay—my mother had voted for him—but we liked Ike even better. If we knew Harry as the man who'd dropped the atomic bomb on the Japanese, we knew General Eisenhower as the man who'd beat Hitler, and I saw him with my own eyes when he drove through Wheeling in an open-topped car. In his pictures, Eisenhower had a smile that was warm, wide, sunny, and inviting. The living man, as I saw him for a second or two, had a smile that could light up the universe.

On February 9, 1950, when I was just a few weeks short of my eighth birthday, Senator Joseph McCarthy made his famous speech—"I have here in my hand a list . . ."—and with it, kicked off the putrid era that bears his name. He made that speech in Wheeling, my home town, but I wouldn't hear a word about it until I was sitting in a lecture hall at West Virginia University some twelve years later—which tells me something about how detached my family was from such matters. My grandmother had a rule that we were not to discuss either religion or politics when we had company, and the one time we did was so unusual that I remember not only the emotional tone—politely angry, mildly distressed—but something of the content. My mother had liked FDR because he was for the working people. "That might be true," my uncle Addison said, "but only the Republicans understand the small businessman."

My father began working at the Hanford nuclear plant in 1947, the year I turned five. He'd learned his skills as a draftsman at Carnegie Tech, had perfected them working for the huge engineering firm of Sanderson & Porter. During the war, he must have been cleared to work on secret projects. He pasted into his scrapbooks only one reference to his day job—a pen and ink drawing so anomalous that it jumped right off the page at us. He'd made a clear, simple, easy-to-understand drawing of a "LIQUID METAL FAST BREEDER

REACTOR (LMFBR)," labeled all of its parts, and signed it "E. C. Maillard."

"Creepy," Mary said.

Within months of arriving in Richland, Gene had clearly established himself as the number one song-and-dance man and all-purpose clown in town. Composing on a "collapsible" organ, he wrote "Our Richland," a song that told the story of the building of the Atomic City, a song approved by the General Electric Company suggestion department. In a substantial run of doggerel, he gave his impressions of living in a dormitory in Building 760. Here's how it begins:

> I'm here in Richland
>> It's been six months
> I'll say myself
>> I'm over the bumps.
>
> My first impression
>> Was none too sweet
> To the barracks I went
>> For the first nine weeks.
>
> My roomie was tall
>> His bunk too short
> His blanket too small
>> It made him snort.
>
> So all night long
>> He fussed and fumed
> And boy! What a snore
>> It should be tuned.
>
> When at 5 AM
>> He silently rose

Started groping about
    To find his clothes.

Then he bumped the chair
    Knocked over the light
I muttered to myself
    Boy! What a night.

Richland declared the first week of September 1948 as Atomic
Frontier Days. Celebrity guests Roddy MacDowell, the Cisco
Kid, and John Wayne entertained, with Rudy Vallee as the master
of ceremonies. The Junior Chamber of Commerce produced a
brochure to mark the occasion.

The cover of the brochure is illustrated with a crude silhouette-
style drawing in red and black—the skyline of a booming town
with smoke rising from smokestacks, a great flare of whiteout at
the center, the whole works crowned with an atom, its electrons
zipping in orbit around the dot of the nucleus. The white
nothingness that represented nuclear power is firing straight lines
of white in all directions and hangs over rolling hills where a chuck
wagon and three men on horseback are making their way across an
empty desert spotted with sagebrush.

Under the heading of "Let's Look Back," the Junior Chamber of
Commerce presents its version of Richland's history.

In the year 1943 a group of men sitting around a table in
Washington, D. C. seriously watched as one of their number
pointed to a tiny spot on a large-scale map of the Pacific
Northwest. Richland! Here, they decided, was the place! Thus
was sown the seed from which sprouted a great plant and a
thriving community.

Within a few months the pastoral quiet of this agricultural

region was no more. Giant bulldozers leveled great tracts of
ground, massive trucks roared day and night along erstwhile
country lanes, new roads appeared and factories exploded
into being from the desert sands. The fantastic barracks town
of Hanford materialized to house thousands of construction
workers. The nucleus of a vast, secret plant, born of wartime
necessity, had been created.

The old farming center of Richland was evacuated and
transformed into a modern community designed to eventually
house thousands of production workers and their families.

Erection of plant and village ended; production of plutonium
began. Only a handful knew "What", and they were not talking.
The village kept its secret well, so well that the nation and the
world first learned of its existence only after the announcement
of the A-bomb.

The Second Annual Atomic Frontier Days was held in August of
1949. The accompanying brochure was no longer free but now
cost twenty-five cents; the cover had changed from red to blue,
from hand-drawn illustration to photography, and featured "hard
hats and assault masks in the northwestern desert." Gene has
pasted a clipping to the front of the brochure—a picture of close
harmony being sung by the Atom City Four and a shot of himself
with the caption: "A soft shoe tap in black face was an Atomic
Frontier Days variety show headliner as done by Jean Millard."

The Richland Chamber of Commerce expressed its gratitude
to the people who made the 1949 Frontier Days a success, and one
of them was my father. Once again, we are given Richland's proud
account of itself.

Scattered deep within this natural isolation are this nation's
most modern industrial plants. The vaunted American mass

production, the assembly line method by which we lead the world in motor cars, in refrigerators, in turbines and egg beaters and pots and pans, is merely a fumbling dress rehearsal compared to the engineering know-how, the construction skill, the unusual operational methods required in this plutonium manufacturing plant.

The product itself, plutonium, is a man-made element which will be usable a thousand years from now for either war or peace. It is a packed power which will not deteriorate with time, which is a million times more powerful than any known fuel. Its manufacturing raises problems of production, storage, worker protection, national security, and world-power-plays, as no other American made package has ever done. It is owned by a free people; it bears a union label.

At the August 1950 Atomic Frontier Days, thirty-five booths were set up in Riverside Park, offering "fun and refreshment." Professional wrestlers went at each other in two exciting matches, and there was also a fireworks display. The Queen of Atomic Frontier Days was crowned, along with her four princesses. And, of course, there was a free variety show—with twenty-three acts that included a comedy routine starring "Tony the Atomic Clown, Little Atom, and Koko, Hydrogen (H20) Bomb." The night ended with the entire cast doing "Baked a Cake."

Gene is listed as one of the directors and appears a number of times in the program, dancing twice with his fifteen-year-old student Gail Muller. He's a year away from turning fifty but in the pictures, looks younger than that—a lean, fit, grinning showman in two-tone oxfords and a theatrical suit. Gail appears in a blazer with nothing under it but sheer tights and tap shoes. Years of dancing have sculpted the muscles in her legs. Two shots catch each of them at the height of a "wing"—balanced in the air with arms flung outward, one foot kicking and the other striking the floor with a toe tap. We can almost hear the laughter and shouting voices egging them on, feel the electrifying exuberance of their performance.

The last photograph in the sequence shows Gene and Gail acting out the story of "Chattanooga Shoe Shine Boy." The image is so crisp that we can see every detail of Gene's hairline moustache. Gail has one foot resting on the top of a folding chair. Gene is polishing her classic black patent tap shoe with a rectangle of cloth. On the bottom of this photo, Gail has written in a schoolgirl's careful hand—"To the nicest and best dancing teacher anyone ever had."

When my father was working there, Hanford's only business was the manufacturing of plutonium for nuclear weapons. Not until 1963—when the N-Reactor added its bit to the Washington Public Power Supply System—would Hanford's nuclear energy be used for any peaceful purpose whatsoever. Hanford officials constantly reassured those employed at the plant, or living near it, that they were perfectly safe, that "not an atom" escaped, but Hanford is the most contaminated nuclear site in North America. It had always discharged radioactive material into the Columbia River and continued to do so until its reactors were decommissioned. It fouled not only the river but the groundwater beneath it and left behind fifty-three million gallons of radioactive waste stored in underground tanks that are leaking. Radioactivity from Hanford has been detected as far away as Oregon, northern California, and southern British Columbia. By 1951, the plant had sent more than 700,000 curies up its smokestacks, most of it in the form of iodine-131. For the sake of comparison, the 1979 Three Mile Island accident released less than 25 curies.

On December 2, 1949—in an exercise called "the Green

Run"—the Hanford Works intentionally released radiation into the atmosphere so that scientists could monitor the resulting radioactive plume and apply that knowledge to the monitoring of Soviet nuclear production. My father—and anyone else living near the Hanford Site—was exposed to twenty times more radiation than the limit allowed by the loose standards of the day. Readings on vegetation afterward were nearly a thousand times over that limit. The Green Run was conducted in absolute secrecy. No one was warned. The public would not know a thing about it for years. By the time that Gene could have first read a newspaper account of the incident, he would have been eighty-five years old.

8.

ON JULY 31, 1997, I interviewed Kippy's father, Loris Brinkman, called "Brink," and a younger man, Carl, in the Travelodge in Delta, British Columbia. The notes I took are sketchy, cursive. Most of what I heard about my father, I wrote down, but large chunks of the interview didn't make it onto the page. I was far from being at my best that night, and the main thing I remember is how surreal it all seemed.

We sat in the room as the daylight faded away and no one bothered to light a light. The TV was on, a bunch of pros playing a game of something, somewhere—baseball? The volume was low. Carl was watching the game, but Brink wasn't. He was talking to me. In the distorting glass of my memory, the scene is set in twilight, lit with the flickering pixels of the TV screen. Brink was friendly enough, helpful enough, but as blunt and straight as a hammer handle. Initially, I read him as a man who had reached an age from which he figured that there was no reason to speak anything other than the plain truth, and I liked him for that.

I see from my notes that Brink had been an engineer. He and his family had moved to Richland in February 1948. Brink had originally worked for DuPont, but his employer kept changing names. DuPont morphed into General Electric, and there were several others—United Nuclear, Martin Marietta, Isocan Rockwell.

When Brink first arrived in Richland, Gene was already there working as a draftsman. He lived alone and avoided crowds because he didn't want to "get a bug." Later he bought a little two-story apartment building in Kennewick, lived upstairs, called it "the Maillard building." Brink laughed at that—at Gene's seemingly boundless ego—and so did I. Gene had terrible allergies that gave him puffy eyes and a stuffy nose most of the year. When he moved to Escondido, he told everyone that he was going for the climate.

Gene "performed tap dancing"—yes, that's exactly what I wrote down, so that's how Brink must have put it. He'd told Brink a story from his early days on stage. Gene was in a comic role, so he used pecan shells to make himself look cross-eyed, but the effect was too realistic. Instead of finding him funny, the audience felt sorry for him. There was nothing worse, he said, than trying to be funny and not getting any laughs, so he worked out another gag. When he made his exit, he was supposed to tip his derby. He lifted it up, and there was another derby under it. He lifted that derby, and there was another one yet—and then another one. The audience gave him a big laugh for that one.

Brink built a little studio in his basement for Kippy. He had to dig out the basement first because it was only half dug when they'd moved in. He finished it and tiled it, and that's where Gene gave Kippy her tap lessons. Gene came every Tuesday night. He charged $2.50 for an hour. Then he'd stay and eat supper with them. As Kippy got older, she gave lessons to other kids in that basement studio.

Carl joined the conversation, and for a while, the two men reminisced about Kippy. I've lost the content of much of this, but I do remember the tone—how proud they were of Kippy

and her accomplishments, how much they valued her opinions—
"You know what Kippy would say about *that*!" Carl said at one
point.

Now that Carl had entered the conversation, he pretty much
took it over. He was a talkative guy. He'd known my father too,
had seen him dance lots of times. Richland had been packed with
remarkable people like my father—interesting, talented people.
It was a nice little town, a great place to grow up. I'd read a lot
about Richland by then, and I agreed with him. Carl said that he
couldn't imagine any other high school anywhere in America that
would have had as many PhDs teaching in it. Yeah, he said, it was
a nice little *conservative* town—making sure I got the point.

"When I was growing up," I told him, "I imagined my father
dancing like Fred Astaire."

Carl laughed at that. "Oh, no. He wasn't like Fred Astaire at all.
He wasn't a thing like Fred Astaire. He did fast tap dancing, really
athletic stuff . . . definitely athletic. If you had to compare him to
somebody, he was more the Gene Kelly type."

I wanted to bring Brink back in, so I asked him if there was
anything else he remembered about my father. Gene had talked
a lot about his experience working in the steel mills, Brink said.
It was hot, hard work. His granddad had worked in the mills too.

Hey, now wait a minute, I thought. Louis Maillard had not
worked in a steel mill. "They were glassblowers," I said.

"Oh?" Brink said.

"The Maillards. They were glassblowers."

Brink gave me a dubious look. "Gene never mentioned that.
Never heard anything about glassblowing." That stopped me.
My mother had always told me that they were glassblowers. The
Montreal phone directory for 1908 had listed Louis Maillard as
a glassblower.

"Did Gene talk about his wives?"

"Well, he had three wives. He didn't talk about them too much. One couldn't be without her mother. She wrote to her mother every day. If she didn't get a letter from her mother every day, she'd get upset. She'd say, 'I didn't get a letter. I have to call her.' Gene asked her, 'Do you want to live with me, or do you want to live with your mother?' She said, 'I want to live with my mother.'"

That was *my* mother—I'd recognized her instantly. I waited to hear the rest of the story, but there was no rest of the story. Could my mother have actually said something like that? If she did say it, maybe it had been on the day she'd left him.

"Gene knew you were a writer," Brink said.

"Oh? . . . Kippy told me that. I've been wondering how he knew that."

"I don't know."

"Did he ever talk about reading anything I'd written?"

"No, he didn't."

Before I could find another question, Brink said, "Gene had the impression you didn't want to see him."

"That's not true. I did want to see him."

"Well, that's not the impression he had."

I'd known right from the beginning that there was something going on below the surface, and I couldn't ignore it any longer. I kept coming up against a hard edge in this man. Gene and Brink had worked together, had known each other for years. They'd been friends. I now read Brink as very much on Gene's team, so what did that make me? Some unknown guy who'd arrived too late, appearing out of nowhere to ask a lot of dumb questions? It was as though Brink felt it was his duty to present Gene's point of view as clearly and firmly as possible. "He thought your mother had poisoned you against him," Brink said.

"Maybe she did," I said. "I know she tried to do that, but . . ." I made an expansive gesture. "Here I am."

"He had cancer, you know . . . testicular cancer. He had a testicle removed. The day he got out of the hospital, he got into his car and drove into the desert. His car broke down. He got stuck in the desert. He had to walk back. It was right after the operation."

I didn't know what to say.

"We could never figure out why he'd done it," Brink said. "It seems like an odd thing to do . . . to drive off into the desert the day you get out of the hospital."

We must have talked about other things after that, but I can't remember them. The last entry in my notebook might have been the last thing Brink said—"Gene always talked low. I never heard him raise his voice."

Talking to Brink had been as close as I was going to get to talking to Gene, and it had badly shaken me. For days afterward, I woke up feeling not right—a particularly nasty variety of not right that's like waking up sickened by the stench of bad breath and realizing that it's your own. I felt as though I had received a message directly from my father—one that predated the "fuck you" he'd sent me in his will. If I was going to continue the conversation, what was I going to say back to him? I'm sorry about the letter I wrote to you when I was twenty? All I could remember about the letter was how angry I'd been when I'd written it. Gene would have been sixty-one when he got it—if he got it. He was still working at Hanford then. He might have talked to Brink about it. I hated the thought, but maybe that was the only real chance I'd ever had to connect with my father.

I knew why Gene had driven into the desert the day he'd got out of the hospital. I understood it because I would have done exactly the same thing. Walking in the desert with one ball, Gene had been thinking about me, I was certain of that. How the hell do you get testicular cancer? I didn't have a clue, but I suspected that being dosed with several hundred thousand curies of radioactive iodine probably didn't help.

I was getting to know my father. I'd studied everything in his black scrapbook, had begun to construct a timeline for him. There were holes in the chronology, but I had a good sense of where he'd been and what he'd been doing for most of his life. When my new-found half-cousin Frank Wade visited us in Vancouver, I interviewed him. Frank gave me a copy of a set of audio tapes Gene had made for his family in the 1980s—Gene singing and doing recitations. From the archives at West Virginia University, I bought a copy of the record made of the Wheeling Steel Hour in 1938 when Gene had appeared on the show. Now I knew what Gene's voice had sounded like both in his forties and in his eighties. The sum of all these bits and pieces was beginning to coalesce into a person.

I played the tapes again, starting with the recitations, listened to that distinctive, resonant, slightly nasal voice, and felt again an eerie sense of familiarity. And then the obvious hit me— Gene sounded like me. His voice was higher pitched than mine, a baritone and not a bass; he didn't have my accent, but he had a timbre much like mine.

A "monologist" Gene called himself, and he certainly did have one hell of a delivery. He employed the old-fashioned declamatory style that must have been heard on the stages of high school gymnasiums all over America, circa 1916. Well, if he'd trilled his Rs, so had Ezra Pound, I thought, but still . . . As I listened to that smoked and salted, well-cured ham, braying and moaning, singing out his vowels, I thought, oh, my God, I'm listening to *my father*.

You really have to work at it to screw up the meter in a Robert W. Service poem, but he manages to do it. In Gene's versions of "The Shooting of Dan McGrew" and "The Cremation of Sam McGee," the strongly built-in rhythms vanish behind the expressive

rubato of his performance—"With ooonly the hoooooooowl of
a timberrrrr wooooolf . . . cleeean MAAAAAD for the MUUCK
called GO-WAL-ED!" As he's playing a drunk in "The Curse
of Drink," Gene can't deliver a line without stuttering on every
consonant, adding a burp or a hiccup, gurgling and bubbling and
wailing. The first time I'd tried to listen to this one, I hadn't been
able to do it. Now I gritted my teeth and let it play through to the
end. It would, I thought, have been easier to listen to a slow-motion
recording of a man drowning in olive oil.

In "I Hunt the Skunk," he's doing a French-Canadian accent,
and it's creditable enough, but it's not what I'd expected, something
any good Canadian comedian could do in half a second—a send-up
of a *genuine* Québécois accent. Instead, it's an American's notion of
a Québécois accent. How odd, I thought, for someone who spoke
French. I liked him best in "Here Come de Judge." I had no way
of knowing whether he'd got that old proto-rap number from
the ancient vaudeville grab bag of his youth or from more recent
versions, but he does it with authority and élan. I felt as though I
were eavesdropping on an early vaudeville performance.

I turned the tape over and listened to the two Christmas songs
he'd written himself. One is an account of how Clement Moore
wrote "A Visit from St. Nicholas" to cheer up his son; the other is
a simple pop tune, built of the most trivial of musical and literary
clichés, about going to Grandma's house on Christmas Eve. He
sings eight other songs on that tape.

"Gene had certain theories about singing," Frank had told me.
"He said the tongue, instead of being flat, should be u-shaped. Your
mouth should be open, not just partially open. You're singing from
back in here," gesturing to his throat, "not up in here," gesturing
to his nose. "He could carry a tune, but you couldn't compare him
to Perry Como or Frank Sinatra or Vic Damone or some of those
fellas." That was putting it mildly. For the most part, Gene sounds

as though he's been frozen in time, lost somewhere back in the 1920s. Forget Frank Sinatra, Gene sings like a man who's never heard of Bing Crosby.

He's in tune most of the time, and that's hard to do when you're singing a cappella and attempting harmonically complex material like "Smoke Gets in Your Eyes," "On a Dreamer's Holiday," or "I Left My Heart in San Francisco." He engages in extravagant vocal swoops, some of which he nails and some of which he doesn't, employs a thick vibrato, and belts out the songs so they could carry easily to the back of any stage. It's a voice designed for turn-of-the-century operetta—an utterly ridiculous voice. He does slightly better in "Zip-a-Dee-Doo-Dah," the pseudo-minstrel song from the now suppressed Disney movie *Song of the South*, but in the Harold Arlen tune "Happy as the Day Is Long," he finally comes into his own. He throws away the hammy vocal production and gives us a song-and-dance man's easy-going delivery just a notch above talking—and sounds, for the first time, like somebody singing something in a way that somebody else might conceivably pay to hear.

He'd done the same song when he'd appeared on the Wheeling Steel Hour broadcast in 1938, so I played the tape from the West Virginia University archives. Gene is now forty-seven, but he sounds as youthful as a man in his twenties. "Happy as the Day Is Long" is an off-the-cuff, laid-back tune, and that's the way Gene does it—light and breezy, no big deal—just the way it should be done. He goes though the tune once, and then he begins to dance.

They must have used different metal in taps in those days; Gene's taps make a muffled, slightly dull sound rather than the bright, sharp clicks we've become used to, but that doesn't matter. Gene is delivering a million taps to the minute. He's tapping rhythmically, accurately, as fast as you can possibly imagine.

Several times the audience bursts into spontaneous applause, and I thought how odd that they should have put a dance performance *on the radio*. There's a picture from this performance—he's been caught in the air, one toe tapping and the rest of him in motion, blurring out, moving too fast for the shutter. It's true—he could really tap up a storm.

"Did you see him dance?" I'd asked Frank Wade when he'd been visiting us.

Oh, often. I took tap dance lessons from him. But I didn't take a lot of them, and I wasn't very good, but he was a really . . . I don't know how to express it. I've seen Arthur Duncan on the Lawrence Welk Show, and he's a good dancer, but he was not as good as Gene. Gene was a marvelous dancer, and he loved to dance. I can remember him telling us when he had his apartment in Escondido, he would dance every day.

Every time he came to visit us, he'd dance with the kids and us. The last time he was here, we didn't have any music that worked for tap dancing, so he just danced without music.

You see this scrapbook. That was only a part of it. He loved to produce shows. He participated as well as produced them. He was good.

Rhythm was important to him. He'd work in these various steps through the rhythm. That's why he liked music that was chorded. He liked the chords because then he could get the rhythm in time. He had to have the sound of the taps to get the rhythm. He did difficult steps . . . some jumps. He worked close to the floor. He was never real low, but he did jumps, and he did buck-and-wings . . . which I thought was difficult as hell. I wouldn't even try to explain it to you.

He was a good ballroom dancer. An excellent ballroom dancer. But his love was tap dancing.

I must have listened to the Wheeling Steel Hour Tape a dozen times before I heard something that had been there all along. When the radio announcer introduces Gene, he pronounces our last name exactly the way my mother said it and exactly the way I still say it—"Muh-lard." Where had my mother and the announcer learned that pronunciation? From Gene, obviously. So our name had once been Anglicized, but years later Gene changed the pronunciation, restored it to its French origins. He told his Masonic brothers it was "My-yard."

This tiny, seemingly trivial bit of information added up with others to give me a new spin on the story. Gene Maillard was a man who'd reinvented himself. In the Ohio Valley, he'd been Gene "Muh-lard" who came from a family of French *glassblowers*. By the time he arrived in Richland, Washington, he'd become Gene "My-yard" who came from a family of French *steelworkers*. Why had he changed the pronunciation of his name to make it more authentic while also, paradoxically, making up an entirely fictitious profession for his family?

Could Gene have ever worked in a steel mill? What had Frank Wade said on the topic? "Gene worked at Wheeling Steel, the Steubenville plant, but he was working in the office, not as a common laborer." Of course Gene hadn't worked as a common laborer. That work was brutal, and he was simply too small a man for it. He would never have been hired; if he had been, he wouldn't have lasted an hour. But they did use boys in glassblowing; I'd seen their pictures—grimy urchins grinning at the camera. If Gene had experienced hot dirty work firsthand, it must have been in a glass plant, so why hadn't he said so? If he'd wanted to emphasize his working-class origins, what was wrong with glass?

I knew all about taking bits and pieces of yourself and using them to create fictional people—I could even say that I was an expert at it—and I was catching my father in a dozen small instances in which he'd created a fictional Gene Maillard who resembled him but wasn't him. If my main purpose was to debunk the fictional creation Gene had made of himself, then I'd never understand him, and I wanted to understand him. As different as we were, I felt an arcane parallel between his life and mine—as though I could learn to read him from reading myself, or perhaps learn to read myself better by reading him. Who *was* the man under the derby, under the derby, under the derby?

9.

"ON THE 21ST OF OCTOBER, 1999, at the Shriners Hospital for Children in Los Angeles, I was presented with a beautiful walnut plaque commemorating my father's generous bequest to that organization. The event was particularly meaningful for me because I never knew my father, Eugene Maillard. For most of his life my father dedicated the creative part of himself to teaching children, and some of his students later became his lifelong friends. He loved children, and his final bequests clearly reveal that love."

That's the way I opened the short account that I wrote—because Gus Klammer had asked me to write it—for the Masonic newsletter, the *Albahr Meter*, published in "the Desert of California, Oasis of San Diego."

It pleased me that the Masonic brethren saw California as a desert. I did too—at least the part of California where my father had spent his last years. I've been places where the landscape looked utterly alien to me—Donegal, the Canadian Prairies, Zacatecas in Mexico—but each had its own peculiar beauty. Nothing around Escondido looked right. What on earth were those bizarre trees? Some of them stuck straight up like enormous toothpicks with circular exclamations of green on top; others grew thick knobby lumps of bark like the scales on an armadillo. In the hills that twisted around unpleasantly like recurring bad dreams, all traces of grass had been seared to beige. The sun, unremitting, slaughtered the world daily, and Gus Klammer hurled us down the California highways with the wholehearted flamboyance of a man who has decided, long ago, that all roads do indeed belong to him. Behind the wheel of a car, he was not merely hard of hearing, he was deaf as a post, and his vision at eighty-eight wasn't quite everything it ought to be either. "Aren't we going a little fast?" I yelled at one point.

"I'm the driver," Gus told me happily, "and you're the passenger."

Since I'd agreed to come to Los Angeles to accept the commemorative plaque, I'd found myself thinking about *the money* in a serious way and wondering, how much? Gus had sent me a copy of the eulogy he'd read at Gene's funeral, and I'd glanced at it—looking for *the story*—and shoved it into a file. I've always had a disregard for numbers that borders on dyslexia, so it wasn't until after I'd organized the information in Gene's scrapbooks that I went back and read the eulogy again and finally got the point.

Gene had seventeen life insurance annuities; they'd been paying about $20,000 a month. Over the years, Gene had given $2,000,000 to the York Rite Knight Templar Eye Foundation, $100,000 to Pasco Commandery Number Twenty-One, $1,278,000 to Consuelo Lodge, $175,000 to the Shriner Hospital for Children, and $35,000 to the Escondido DeMolay. At the time of his death, Gene had $750,000 in his accounts. Holy crap, that was a lot of money! That was over four million bucks.

I had no doubt that Gene had loathed me and my mother every time he'd signed his name to the checks he'd sent us. If he started in 1943 and stopped in 1960, that added up to about $2,200—which, compared to four million bucks, was fairly pathetic. But maybe it wasn't fair to think of it that way. To make an honest comparison, in the 1950s, that amount would have sent a kid to college or bought half a house.

I didn't take very good notes. Simply being there at all, moving through my father's space, used me up, and some days I didn't write a thing. I remember Gus driving. California throughways unwind in my memory without any clear focus, with no more substance than a video game—like the dogged images that cycle through your head when you're halfway between waking and sleeping, when your mind's still logging off—yet with a creepy sparkle of danger. I remember sitting in Gus's apartment at night, neither of us quite ready for bed yet. It was the perfect time for a drink, but neither of us were drinkers. We talked until we were yawning.

Gus's business card says, "Canadian-born Californian, American by choice." He'd grown up in a religious community in Bruderheim, Alberta; he was vague on exactly what religion, although he did remember that doctrinal matters were so important to the folks who lived there that they split into two warring factions, each excommunicating the other. When the Spanish Influenza pandemic struck his part of Alberta, Gus had been seven years old. It was bitterly cold, and Gus was sick as a dog, running a high fever, deathly ill. His father sent a message into town for the doctor who eventually came by in his sleigh. Gus's father was out in the barn milking the cows. The doctor said, "I've already filled out the death certificate for him . . . left it on the kitchen table. All you have to do is write in the exact time when he dies," and he drove off to see someone else. The doctor had a whole stack of death certificates with him.

Gus's father was furious. "No, dammit, he's not going to die." He went to see their neighbors on the next farm, the Ukrainians—or, as Gus pronounced it, "the Uk-er-rainians"—and he got some of that fine red Uk-er-rainian whiskey, brought it back, mixed it with sugar and fed it to Gus in little drops. Gus made it through the night. "And here I am," he said, laughing.

I'd brought pictures of Elizabeth to show him. Of course I'd picked ones of her tap dancing. "It's a shame Gene didn't know her," Gus said. "Don't you think he would have loved his little granddaughter? Of course he would. He would have adored her." Then he said again something he said so often it became a leitmotif—*"You were so easy to find!"* Studying the pictures, he said, "He would have wanted to leave her something. I know he would."

Gus was determined that I was going to see as much of Gene's life as he could show me. The first night I was in Escondido, he took me to the Masonic lodge where Gene had been a member. There, in the Eugene C. Maillard Lodge Room, was the huge oil painting of my father that Gus had paid for. Based on a photograph, it presents my father as an old gent in a natty herringbone suit with matching fedora. The bland, efficient brushstrokes of the anonymous painter have transformed Gene into *The Donor*. He's smiling slightly—giving him the small-eyed, sphinxlike, faintly benevolent expression of the pint-sized alien in the first science fiction movie I ever saw, *The Man from Planet X*. We walked in, looked up, saw Gene looking down at us, and Gus stopped in his tracks. The intensity of his emotion obviously took him by surprise, and the words burst out of him: "I loved the man!"

As much as I'd learned about my father by then, I couldn't improve upon the summary of him that Gus had written into his eulogy: "Gene was a very unusual man—extremely hardworking, honest and kind, yet tight and cheap." I particularly appreciated the way Gus's sentence turned on the word "yet."

The mean-spirited miser who wore the same suit for forty years and resented contributing gas money to his friends was not a man I could like very much, but I admired the entertainer. "We've got to brighten up the old folks," he'd said to Kippy, and he'd brightened up more than the old folks. In his last years, he hadn't been thinking about nuclear weapons or General Electric; he'd been thinking about the kids he'd taught, the times when he'd stepped out onto the stage and made people laugh. That was the man I wished I'd known—the showman, the clown, the teacher.

Sitting at Gus's kitchen table, I read Gene's obituary again. The three column inches informed me that he'd died "at his home." A high-end elder care facility might not be what we usually think of as home, but, in the end, that was the only home that Gene had.

"Maillard is survived by his friends. There are no surviving family members."

Survived by his friends? That had a nicely defiant ring to it. The fifty or so Masons who'd shown up for Gene's funeral had been friendly acquaintances. The people who stick with you right to the end are the ones who are your friends, and Gene had been survived by two of them—Gus and Kippy. Gene had died, cared for by paid staff, looked after by a Masonic brother, and visited by his best student.

"What about his nephew, Frank Wade?" I asked Gus. "He was a surviving family member . . . and a close one too. Gene lived with Frank and Olga Wade off and on for years back in the 30s."

"All I know is what Gene told me. When he got sick and wasn't expected to live, I said, 'Do you want me to contact anybody, Gene? What about that Doctor Wade?' And he said, 'No, you don't have to worry about that doctor.'"

"That doesn't make sense," I said. "The last trip that Gene made, he went to see Frank and Joy Wade in Williamsport. He crossed the country in a Greyhound bus to do it. He recorded songs and recitations for them. He dedicated his Christmas song to Frank and Joy. So what happened?"

Gus shook his head. "I don't know. He told me he had no use for 'that Dr. Wade.'" He imitated the dismissive sneer in Gene's voice.

Frank must have appeared to be a little too interested in Gene's money, I thought, but I didn't want to get into that with Gus.

Gene had disowned most of his family after his mother had died, and then, at the end of his life, he'd disowned the only little bit of family he had left. How sad. "Did he think everybody wanted his money?" I asked.

"I don't know. He had an unhappy childhood. I've told you all about that."

We'd reached the point where we were recycling Gene's stories—maybe in the hope that they'd fall into a new pattern that would make everything make sense. "He talked about getting divorced three times," Gus said. "Every divorce cost him money . . . Say, was your mother real young when she married him?"

"Well, not really. Late twenties."

"I thought she might have been real young. Gene said she couldn't leave her mother . . . We didn't know he had a son. The first we heard of it was when Tom was drawing up his will. It took us all by surprise."

"Maybe he didn't need a family," I said. "The Masons were his family."

"That's true. We probably were. But not too many Freemasons visited him in his last years, shame to say. I took on the responsibility of looking after him. I did the best I could . . . at no charge. I'm not taking an executor's fee, you know, not a penny. I'm planting a seed, and I hope to reap the harvest."

That, I thought, must be the Masonic version of the law of karma, but it didn't strike me as unreasonable to expect someone who's worth millions to leave at least something to his executor—especially to one like Gus. But now I found a new way to look at it. If Gus had ever taken a penny, then Gene couldn't have been absolutely certain that Gus was a *real* friend.

Yes, there was something sad about all of this—and crazy. I mean pathological, genuinely nuts. Gene had cut himself off from all family connections—from anyone who might have a claim on him—and he'd worked like a dog, scrimped and saved, denied himself, and he'd done it all to make money. In a culture that defines a man by his money, he'd made himself into a millionaire—and for a poor boy from Pittsburgh, that was a hell of an accomplishment—and then he'd given all of it away like a great chief at a potlatch, *and not one penny of it to anyone he knew personally*. Yes, it was crazy, but there was also, I had to admit, something magnificent about it too. What a huge, splashy, larger-than-life gesture. I still didn't know exactly what Gene had meant by that gesture, but it was magnificent nonetheless.

The next morning, as I was writing up my notes, Gus said, "I'll be right back, *Gene*. I'm just going down to check the mail."

Gus drove us to San Diego to meet Kippy. Her husband, Gary, was harbormaster at a hotel marina. He sat and made small talk with us until Kippy arrived—stepping into the scene just late enough to have given herself a small, deft character entrance. She was blond, perfectly put together, elegant and casual—in navy slacks, a white top, and navy scarf with gold stripes that gave her a young, fresh, sailor-girl look. I knew from reading Gene's newspaper clippings exactly how old she was; she looked easily ten or fifteen years younger than that, and I had no trouble believing that she'd been a Miss America contestant.

I could have made notes in the hotel restaurant, but that would have distanced me, and I decided that simply being there was more important. I was hearing in person the slow, warm, easy, sympathetic voice I'd heard on the telephone. Both Kippy and her husband were models of graciousness, but she and I made each other nervous—or maybe I was nervous and made her nervous. I'm not sure what the dynamic was, but I remember the intensity of it. I wanted something from her, and it must have showed.

I'd brought leftover pictures that Gus had found. One was of

Kippy as a girl of eleven, in a shiny dance costume, skating into a crowded room with Gene standing behind her. "That's the routine where I tapped on roller skates," she said. The skates were the old clip-on kind. Twice she pointed out to me the drums in the back of the picture. She and Gene tapped out the rhythm on the snare drum—then danced it. In another picture she was even younger—six or seven—doing a tap routine with "a real boxer's skip rope," she told me. In a small, square, color shot, Kippy had grown up. She was standing with one of her own tap students and with Gene—an impossibly fit-looking man in his seventies.

Gene had taught tap in routines, Kippy told me, a first-level routine, and a second, and a third, and so on. She'd used the same method when she'd been teaching. He'd emphasized opposite arms, a graceful carriage, didn't want the arms simply hanging there, and she illustrated for me, showing me motionless arms held stiffly at her sides—like an Irish dancer, I thought. He'd taught her a beautiful soft-shoe routine. She'd forgotten it and had to ask him to teach her again when she met him later, when she herself had become a tap teacher. She asked me if I wanted her old tap records, the ones she'd used when she was first learning with Gene. I said, "Yes, of course."

As we talked, I felt a growing tension almost to the point of being depersonalized, watching myself form sentences to speak. I wanted to connect with her—my father's best student—to make a link back to Gene Maillard who'd been floating just behind my shoulder ever since I'd arrived in California. What I wanted was simple and impossible—to embody myself into my dead father's life, and he into mine, interlinking our lives like the parallel worlds in a science fiction story. I wanted an inner clarity, but it was eluding me.

Kippy told me again the story of playing for Gene "as he was failing," playing "Tea for Two," saying, "Remember when we used to dance to this, Gene?" He didn't speak, but she had the sense that her voice was "going in somehow." She squeezed his hand, felt him squeeze hers back. Maybe he opened his eyes. She described him in his last days as "shrunken down to a shell"—getting smaller and smaller. Telling me the story, she made a gesture of closing in, folding in, minimizing. The next night he died.

Near the end of the lunch, I remember us both standing, our eyes nearly level. Her eyes met mine and held. I saw her, or imagined that I could see her, working hard to give me something. Kippy seemed to me not only a deeply intuitive person but someone with a talent far larger than that—a talent for going out and meeting people where they are. She answered the question that I hadn't been able to ask her—or even to form clearly to myself. "Your dad was a good man, Keith."

I couldn't say anything.

"Even if he wasn't smiling," she said, "your dad always had a little twinkle in his eye, like he was just getting ready to smile."

The night before I was leaving, Gus asked me if I wanted Gene's things in the display case. "Sure," I said, "they'd be nice to have someday."

But no, Gus didn't mean someday—he meant *right now*. "I can't take that stuff," I said. "It wouldn't be right. What about your heritage? What about your traditions?"

When we got to the lodge, there was no one there but us. "You want the display case too?" he said. "It's a great case. It's worth at least three hundred dollars."

"Well, I'm not sure how I'd get it on the plane."

Gus unlocked the case and began stuffing Gene's sacred objects into the carton he'd brought with him. "I don't know about this, Gus," I said. "What about *your traditions*?"

He pointed up at the wall where the pictures of Past High

Priests were displayed. "Those are the men that knew Gene. Most of them are gone now."

From one entire wall and half of another, old dead Masons looked down on us. "The young guys don't care," Gus said. "Aw, we might as well take the case too," and then an eighty-eight-year-old Shriner and a fat guy with a bad back were hauling that heavy sucker out of the Masonic lodge at 11 o'clock at night and roping it into the trunk of the car. What happened to the display case I have no idea, but everything else accompanied me on the plane back to Vancouver. As I was leaving, Gus gave me a sheet of paper with what looked like an odd free-verse poem printed on it.

PRESS ON

Nothing in the world can take the place of persistence.
Talent will not; nothing is more common
than unsuccessful men with talent. Genius will not;
unrewarded genius is almost a proverb. Education will not;
the world is full of educated derelicts. Persistence and
determination alone are omnipotent.

[Signed in handwriting] *Gus Klammer*

Back home, I checked on the net to see if Gus might have been quoting from somebody, and I discovered, to my surprise, that those were the words, slightly rearranged, of Calvin Coolidge. I've liked some American presidents better than good old taciturn Cal, but he's not the worst of the lot—not by a long shot—and it seemed appropriate that my last message from Escondido should be a voice from the twenties. And it wasn't bad advice either.

10.

I DIDN'T FEEL LIKE DISPLAYING my walnut plaque from the Shriners Hospital, but I liked some of the things from Gene's display case—his golden chalice that looked like the Holy Grail as it's often represented in Pre-Raphaelite paintings and his glass pyramid that resembled the strange one with the eye that appears on the American one-dollar bill. I arranged those arcane objects on top of our piano in front of a framed picture of my mother, holding me, as a baby, in her arms. Within a day, the picture mysteriously jumped off the piano, the glass shattering into a million pieces. "You should have known better," Mary said. "You shouldn't have put your mother and father together."

I wanted to do something for Gene—and for myself. I wanted to find a way to make peace with him—to bless him, to lay him to rest. Okay, I thought, I'll have my own funeral for him. I found my copy of *The Book of Common Prayer*. Standing alone in my bedroom, I read the "Service for the Burial of the Dead" for him. The words of the Psalm fit for both of us: *"For I am a stranger, and a sojourner, as my father was."*

I felt as though I had completed something important, that I could get on to the next phase of my life, but I still had to catalog the last of the relics. I began to sort through the packages that Gus had sent me, found Gene's passport information, his social security card, his wallet—object after object. So difficult a thing I was asking myself to do—trying to imagine what he would have thought if he'd known that I would have these things spread out around me on my bed in Vancouver, British Columbia.

Then I found a single scrap of yellow lined paper marked with Gus's distinctive handwriting. It appeared to be either a draft of a letter that Gus had sent to the Shriners Hospital about the presentation of the memorial plaque or, perhaps, notes he'd made for himself before he'd decided to contact me about it.

"In no way will we include a wife," Gus had written. "Noble Gene was divorced about 54 years ago. Noble Gene has not seen his only son Keith since the boy was three years. *And wanted no part of him.*"

How could a few scribbled words hit me so hard? Those words made me sick. It was as though I'd been ambling through the woods like a naïvely trusting L'il Abner and had stepped on a corpse. A demonic toggle switch in my mind had been thrown; with a single click, everything was reversed. Nauseated and sweating, trying to gulp it down—I walked in circles in our yard, thinking, *that can't be right, that can't be right, that can't be right.* But of course it was right. Why had I expected anything else? Wasn't that always what I'd got from him—nothing? Sick? Oh, I was sick, all right. I'm bloody well sick of *you*, Gene, I thought—you bizarre egomaniac.

Gus hadn't been merely Gene's executor, he'd been Gene's best friend, so he must have felt justified in making a leap from what Gene had said he wanted to what Gene might have wanted if he'd still been around. There was no doubt that Gus Klammer liked me, and I was glad of that. Gus Klammer was one of the finest men I'd ever met. But my own honest-to-God biological father had wanted no part of me and had said so.

What had he known about me? Had he read any of my books? The one most readily available in the United States would have been *Alex Driving South*, a gritty West Virginia tale full of four-letter words—and a man of his generation would have cringed at every one of them—but it had been published by a major New York house and had received good reviews. Surely that would have counted for something.

Then there was the damnable letter I'd written when I was twenty. Brink had told me that Gene thought my mother had poisoned my mind against him, and maybe he'd used my letter as evidence. But I was getting tired of trying to see things from Gene's point of view. What about *my* point of view? I'd been in a no-win situation. It wouldn't have made any difference what I'd written to him when I was twenty. He'd poisoned his own mind against *me*.

If my mother had hated his guts—and she had—then Gene had hated her guts too. Without knowing much of anything about me, he'd wanted no part of me. But that didn't have a thing to do with me—it was between Gene and my mother, something that had happened in that mythical unknowable place called "Hot Springs, Arkansas." I was going to stop blaming myself for it. He'd been the adult—why the hell hadn't he acted like one?

For months I kept poking around in my notes, adding a few lines here and there, still keeping up a pretense that I might write a book, or maybe a personal essay. I kept thinking that I should be able to make *something* out of it—otherwise, why had I gone to all that trouble? But what could I possibly write? I'd been spinning a web of fiction—a poeticized, sentimental, soft-focus tale about a grown-up boy searching for his father and finding him—and it was all lies. I wasn't going to get tricked into doing that again.

Eventually I filed the whole lot of it away and did my best to forget it. The short obligatory public statement I'd written for the *Albahr Meter* seemed to have exhausted everything I had to say. I could look back at my life and detect the absence of a father in the black hole—but so what? I felt as though there was a core to my experience so dark and personal that I could never communicate it to anyone. Why should I try to write about Gene Maillard? I'd never had a father. I didn't have one now.

One night a couple of years later, I checked my emails and found an odd one appearing out of nowhere, coming from someone I didn't know.

From: J.R.
Sent: Thursday, January 31, 2002 9:23 AM
Subject: Eugene C Maillard

Hello Keith—

I will try to make this message brief. I ran across your Bio on the net, saw that you had lived in Wheeling, West Virginia. The interesting part for me is this: my Birth Father was a Eugene Charles Maillard and lived in Wheeling WV. I have not seen or heard from him since I was 4 years old. My Mother's name was Ruth Grace Jamerson from Pittsburgh Pa, she was born in 1910, died 1984. My name is Robert James Maillard and I was born in Pittsburgh, Pa., in 1931.

This is my first search into looking for my Father, any information from you concerning relative info in this regard would be highly appreciated.

All the Best
Robert Maillard

As she often did in the evenings, Mary was relaxing with a book. I walked upstairs and sat down in the chair by the bed. "I just got an email from Ruth Maillard's kid," I said and handed it to her.

As strange as it might seem, I hadn't got to the heart of it yet, but Mary got there immediately. "Oh, my God, Keith," she said, "he's your brother."

11.

"MY MOTHER WOULD NEVER TALK about him."

"Nothing?" I said.

"Nothing. Just things like he had a dance studio and worked as a draftsman for a railroad or something."

I was trying to place his voice—his age, his accent, his inflection—trying to figure out why it was so evocative, why he sounded so damned familiar. It was an upbeat, affable, hip, streetwise, urban voice—like something from the world of 1950s radio. Then I got it. He sounded a bit like Phil Harris—or at least like the way Harris had sounded on the old Jack Benny show or when he'd done the voice for Little John, the bear, in Walt Disney's *Robin Hood*. "Didn't she tell you anything else?" I said.

He laughed. "Not a damned thing. Whenever I asked her, she'd just give me this icy stare."

That was the clincher—the silence, the ice. Yes, we were talking about the same man—the clown, the trickster, the ham, the goofball, the old-time hoofer vanishing into the wings with his niftiest shuffle-off-to-Buffalo—of course it was Gene Maillard with a twinkle in his eye, leaving behind not one, but *two* pissed-off ex-wives who wouldn't talk about him. I was sure of it now—the guy on the other end of the telephone line had to be *my brother*.

"I don't remember Gene at all," I said. "Do you?"

"Just barely. I remember standing in the bathroom, watching him shave. I remember him taking me out once. I don't think he ever lived with us."

I described Gene's clipping with the pictures of the chorus girl, Mademoiselle Ruth Maillard, sightseeing in Columbus. "Yeah, that's my mother," he said. "I've got that very same clipping. I've got tons of pics. I'll scan some of them and send them to you."

No, he didn't sound like Phil Harris. That had been my first stab at trying to place him, but it wasn't quite right. He was ten years older than I was, so he'd been an actor in that haunting, enormously familiar black-and-white movie that had been playing just before I'd been born, and that's what I was hearing—a voice from the 30s. I'd joined that old movie in the 40s. Our accents were different, but the difference wasn't crucial. There was something about his voice that reminded me of my own.

"Mom wasn't around much," he was telling me. "She'd pop in and out occasionally. She was mostly on the road . . . as a showgirl, a dancer, a cigarette girl, a singer, and various things of that nature. The whole family was involved in show business at one time or another. She was holding up her end . . . because in 1931 you're in the heart of the Depression, so people had to be out there working at all these odd jobs just to bring in money for room and board. I was living with her mother and father . . . turns out later it was her stepfather." His tone said, can you beat that?

He laughed again. "I had the *strangest* family. Everybody hid everything from everybody."

"Yeah? Well, my family was a little on the odd side too."

Gene had provided him with half his genes just as he'd provided me with half of mine. In terms of Maillard blood, that was as close as I was likely to get, and I kept trying to feel a cellular connection to him, something more than an abstract *idea* of kinship. "What should I call you? Bob? Robert?"

"No. You can call me J.R."

As a child, he'd been Robert James Maillard, but nobody had ever called him Robert; he'd been James. Later, when he'd joined the Navy, a lot of the guys on his ship had been James or Jim or Jimmy—so, to avoid confusion, he'd been anointed J.R., and it had stuck. "I always told people that J.R. stood for Just Right. Interestingly enough, the guy who played J.R. on *Dallas* was born on the same day, the same month, and the same year as I was."

For most of his life he'd used his stepfather's last name— Worden. He'd just recently gone back to Maillard. He'd hoped that changing his name back would change his life—and it had. For starters, here he was talking to a brother he'd never known about. "I always wanted a brother," he said.

"Well, you've got one."

For his first seven years J.R. had been raised by his grandparents. His grandmother had been the solid, stable core of his childhood— just as my grandmother had been of mine. His memories of her seemed to be very much a little boy's—he'd loved her for her kindness and her cooking. We discovered that we'd both inherited Gene's health problems—"You too, huh?"—constantly dripping noses, wadded-up handkerchiefs, blinding headaches, rattling coughs, vivid fever dreams. "I was sick so much I almost didn't make it through the first grade," I told him.

"Well, I *didn't* make it. I had to repeat the sucker." He'd done his homework lying on his back because if he tried it sitting up, his nose dripped onto the pages so badly that he had to throw them away. "Did you get tested for allergies?"

"Oh, sure," I said. "For all the good it did me. I'm allergic to cats, horses, house dust, a million different plants . . ."

"I'm allergic to *everything*." We shared a good laugh over our childhood miseries. "Thanks a lot, Gene!" J.R. said.

Unlike me, he'd felt guilty about not trying to find our father.

"I kept wondering about him. What's he up to? What's he doing? I figured the best thing to do was call my grandmother, and she says, well, she'd write a letter to his last known address which would have been in Wheeling, West Virginia, and I says, 'Great,' so she sent off a letter, and it came back from a dead letter office in Wheeling, and that was the end of that."

As we were coming to the end of our conversation, we got around to swapping information about our lives. J.R. had gone into the navy straight out of high school. That was the Korean War, and he'd got close enough to it to have shots fired at him. After he'd got out of the service, he'd worked for several airlines in various capacities from ticketing to management and had developed a great fondness for stewardesses. He'd also done dozens of other things—sold Heathkit radios, promoted audiovisual equipment in Nigeria, renovated houses and flipped them, been an all-purpose handyman, floating around Santa Fe with, as he put it, "a Santa Fe toolkit"—a readiness to do anything that anybody needed, from deep tissue massage to psychic readings. He was into New Age stuff—had a spirit guide who advised him from time to time. He'd never married, although he'd come close. He was now, the best I could tell, retired. That made sense; he was seventy. We both said how weird and wonderful it was to connect after all these years and promised to keep in touch via email.

"Do you like him?" Mary asked me.

"I do. I like him a lot. He's very different from me, but I can feel a connection . . . a lot of stuff going on underneath the words."

I was still thinking about our mutual father. "One thing for sure . . . Gene Maillard had a real talent for pissing off women."

Gene was back in my mind again, so I pulled out my file of dead writing and read it straight through at one sitting. I'd been writing about him, but what about me? Maybe I should be writing about what Gene's absence had meant to me, but how could I write about *not having something*? I was not exactly uninformed about the social problem of absent fathers, and I did have opinions on the topic. Fatherless boys do less well than boys with fathers in nearly every area in which we care to test them, but critics of those studies have pointed out that what we might be finding is the result not of fatherlessness, but of *poverty*.

In terms of giving me a good start in life, my mother and grandmother had done *just fine*—but at a cost. In my mother's last job, she was an office manager, supervising twenty or so "girls" and doing the payroll for a good-sized company. When she asked her boss for a raise, he said, "Aileen, you're already one of the highest paid women in the Ohio Valley." That meant that she was getting paid about what a man would have made in his first entry-level office job. My mother owed her soul to Household Finance. She spent years paying them back. If we want to do something to help fatherless boys, we should start by improving things for working women.

Another thing we should be doing is stop making fatherless boys feel like freaks because they don't come from traditional nuclear families. We've already reached the point at which there are more families in North America that don't match that ideal than ones that do. The very term "nuclear"—as applied to a family of husband, wife, and child—is wrong. The real nucleus of the family is a child and one or more adults to take care of it—and most often those adults are women. We should be celebrating families in all of their forms. We should be shouting, "Hooray for grandmothers!"

Maybe I could write a nonfiction book—a long, argumentative, well-researched personal essay. Sure, that could work. I tried out the idea on my wife.

She gave me a long look that told me what she thought. "What about Gene?" she said.

What about him? Mary was welcome to be interested in him—
he wasn't *her* father—but he didn't feel like mine either. All
he'd left me were his genes, and I knew that fatherhood meant
a hell of a lot more than that because I was a father now myself.
Gene had been lucid right to the end, his lawyer had told me—
lucidly thinking about *what*? Did I need that phone call telling
me that he'd died? No, I did not. I hadn't been thinking about
him then, and I could have happily gone the whole rest of my life
not thinking about him, and the only reason his lawyer had called
me at all was to get my mailing address so he could send me the
only message I would ever receive from my father: "You're getting
nothing."

I was still angry at Gene Maillard, and it was personal. I
could tell myself that it was irrational of me to be angry, that it
was immature, that it was beneath me, but nothing I told myself
would make it go away.

I called J.R. "I'm kind of down," I told him. "I've been trying
to write something or other about Gene . . . God knows what. But
whenever I try to go back to him, I get stuck. I'm really pissed off
at him."

I told him about trying to read the black hole—to read what
wasn't there. I told him how I'd felt like a ghost. I told him about
trying to learn French from Linguaphone records and about the
Canadian flag on my wall. I told him that I didn't know how much
of this related to Gene and how much of it didn't.

He listened to it all, laughed or said a few words in the right
places.

"Did you ever feel abandoned?" I asked him.

"Yeah, I felt . . ." He hesitated a moment. "As shy as I was, I
always wanted to know who he was, and where he was, and like I
told you, the last time I seen him was when I was four years old. I
do remember at least being picked up by him and him taking me

out for the day. And I remember the last time he was supposed
to come by. They dressed me up in a little sailor uniform and put
me down on the stoop on the front of the porch. And he never
showed up."

"Shit."

"I sat there and waited for him all afternoon . . . But I didn't
know how to relate to that pain, the pain of having a father, a very
special person coming to get you . . . and he doesn't show up. There
was a build-up to it, and then there was a no-show, so, yeah, there
was always this . . . and then I spent a lifetime wondering about
him."

Neither of us said anything for a moment. It wasn't an awkward
silence. It felt as though we were letting things settle.

"Do you feel better?" he asked me.

"Yeah, I do."

12.

MY BROTHER COMES FROM A FAMILY so hermetic that it makes mine—with its ancient secrets, unspoken assumptions, and thick layers of cryptic subtext—look like something painted by Norman Rockwell. His grandparents told J.R. that his uncle, Robert—who was only six years older than J.R. and had the same name as he did—was his brother. J.R.'s mom had been on the stage since she was three; she kept her scrapbooks and photographs, but she wouldn't talk about them—in fact, Ruth wouldn't talk about much of anything. J.R.'s grandmother had been on the stage too, but she wouldn't talk about it either. J.R.'s grandfather had once worked as a stagehand for Houdini—maybe.

It wasn't until she was about to emigrate to Canada that J.R.'s mother found out that the man she'd always thought was her real father was actually her stepfather. Her real father was an obscure film grinder named Gustav Bergman, and nobody knew a damned thing about him. Her stepfather, meanwhile, had been flying under an alias; he'd been calling himself Jamerson, but his real name was Shumate. Both J.R.'s grandfather and his stepfather—that is, Peter Worden whose real name was Frederick—were alcoholics who drank daily with the stolid determination of men who are into the bottle for the long haul.

Just as he'd promised, J.R. had sent me photographs of both

himself and of his mother. In her earliest picture, Ruth is a child—a brunette with her hair cut short into a 20s bob, wearing a striped pullover like a boy's, looking not directly at the camera but off to one side with dark eyes. She's so sad it takes me a moment to realize how beautiful she is.

In what must be her high school graduation portrait, Ruth is a lovely well-groomed young lady. Then, later, when the fully adult butterfly emerges, her eyebrows are as sharply inked as etchings, her hair as blond as Jean Harlow's, her lips painted with the dark, intense, unabashedly artificial matte lipstick of her day. She's been transformed into Ruth, the 30s showgirl. The wording on a postcard warns us: "Don't get a ringside seat at a Miami nightclub if you are an attractive male, for your wife, best girl, or someone else's wife may not like the attention paid you by the entertainers." One of the entertainers standing by, an alluring Siren, is Ruth Maillard—at the Frolics Club, Miami, Florida, on March 3, 1937.

The end of the series shows Ruth retired from the stage and married. With her neat little hat and clip-on earrings, her makeup toned down into respectability, she's playing the young matron just as successfully as she'd played any of her previous roles. In none of her adult pictures does she reveal even a flicker of the person behind the mask.

The photographs of J.R. cover a similar span of his life. As a child, he wears a face that's shy, tentative, and strongly resembles childhood pictures of our father. In high school, he looks as much like a stereotype of a clean-cut 40s kid as a character from an Archie comic. In the Navy, in a swimming suit, he's impossibly fit—"ripped," as Liz would say—the muscles on his stomach as clearly defined as the ripples on a washboard. Later, in Santa Fe and Sedona, he's a bearded, long-haired neo-hippie. As an adult, he greets the camera with a what-you-see-is-what-you-get grin and resembles neither me nor Gene. "My God, you were a handsome devil," Mary wrote to him, and it's true.

J.R. came to visit us at Christmas. We sat around at our kitchen table with my tape recorder running, and he told us the story of his life. His voice on the tape ranges through a complex set of emotions. He sounds, in turn, dumbfounded, amused, astonished, and deeply offended.

Nobody ever talked to me. When I tried to find out anything about my family or who I was, all I found was a big hole. Like I couldn't pin anything down. It just vaporized. And I always thought . . . it's *interesting*. It's all tied in. I'm normal weight, normal height. I've got two normal-colored eyes. Normal this, normal that. What I was, was average in every way possible so you could miss me . . . except for this family which was not there at all. I couldn't pin them to anything.

My relationship with my mother was odd. She was like Greta Garbo—an I-want-to-be-alone person. We never had any real conversation. She would talk and not want an answer, and that was about it. It was the most unusual one-way street I ever lived on. You could tell she was a very nice woman, but very private.

Everything had to be in perfect order. Everything had to be on time. I was always forced to eat alone. When we did eat together, I had to know how to use the right fork, the right knife, the right spoon. Everything was totally controlled. I couldn't make any noise. I had to be this perfect being. It was very interesting because it started early in life when we moved to Montréal. They dressed me up in blue blazers and little short gray flannels, perfect shoes, and when we would go out, these rare times to these little restaurants, I had to be the perfect gentleman. I could never talk unless someone talked to me. It was a one-way street. As I look back on it, it was the most interesting thing I've ever been through. I spent a good deal of my time in my room.

She didn't talk about much of anything. If she would say, "Oh, I just read a detective novel," she would talk a little bit about the detective novel and not want any reply from you. It was like news of the day, and it was very short-lived news of the day. Since we had no conversation, I wasn't much of a conversationalist. There was no communication in the household, that I can recall, that was directed at me, so I got very good at sitting and not saying anything. It was quite odd. I always knew that she liked me, but she was never demonstrative. She never hugged me.

J.R.'s grandmother had been the dependable bedrock of his childhood, but when he was seven, he was sent on the train—the maiden run of the Silver Meteor from New York City to Miami—to join his mother and stepfather. I hear him slow down, hesitate, search for words.

Okay, the loss of leaving the real family, as I call it—the grandparents—there was a tremendous loss. Number one, I was a very shy child, never would speak unless spoken to, and I had to drag everything out of me, so the idea of going off with foreigners, so to speak . . . because I really didn't know my mother . . . was a great shock, and to soften the blow, they sent me with my uncle on the streamliner down to Florida, and he would stay the summer with me to help cross that barrier of merging into a new family. And it seemingly worked, because when we got down there, it was a perfect season to learn all about the beaches, and playing in the sand, and chasing seagulls, and things like that,

but it was also a very sad time when the summer was over and my
uncle had to go back to Pittsburgh.

J.R.'s stepfather, Peter Worden, was a Canadian. During the Second
World War, he was an officer in the Canadian Army and stationed
all over the country. He and Ruth took J.R. with them when they
could, dumped him with relatives when they couldn't. By the time
J.R. graduated from high school—a year late—he had passed
through seventeen schools, nine in the States, eight in Canada. His
only uninterrupted year of schooling had been kindergarten.

I listen. He's telling me about the places where he lived, what
he remembers of this school or that, but then he loops back to say
what he has already said about the loss of his family. I've been there
countless times myself—that reprise. It happens with a story of
pain. You keep going back to tell that story again because you're
trying to find a way to tell it so that it will stay told.

It was a bitter pill to take—that loss of my family—and it
amplified over the years because of all the schools I had to endure,
plus all the provinces in Canada and all the schools in the States.
It's never . . . I was always out of sync with any curriculum that the
schools had at that time, so, ah . . . It was like I could not defend
myself to teachers because I could not speak. Someone would ask
me my name, and I could hardly pronounce the name Maillard. It
just wouldn't come out, and the voice was so small, so I have a lot
of inferiority complexes . . . I wouldn't say one complex, a whole
variety of them. That was a great loss. Probably I never got over it.
I was somehow invisible to the world. I was just this person who
almost didn't exist on the surface of life.

My feelings for a real father . . . At that time I had a stepfather
who was . . . He didn't have much to say to me. That's when I
began to explore in my own mind what it would be like to have "a

real father" instead of . . . whatever you want to call a stepfather.
So the reason I wanted a real father, the big thing that played out
over and over, was I literally had no direction.

He wasn't kidding. He's left me with an image of himself and
a buddy in Florida—two fifteen-year-old boys adrift in a twelve-
foot dory. Their standard practice was to pack peanut butter and
jelly sandwiches and go fishing with small lures and light line so
if they caught something big, the fight with the fish would be all
that more exciting. Their ancient wreck of a boat leaked so badly
they had to bring huge pails and take turns bailing, but they
didn't bother to bring oars because they didn't really need them—
they had a one-and-one-tenth horsepower Evinrude motor. They
started from Miami, headed out the Little River Canal, through
the bay, and into the open sea. By midday the sun was fierce. They
both fell asleep and forgot to bail. A huge voice from a megaphone
woke them—"Ahoy down there! Do you need any help?" They
looked up and saw a freighter looming over them. The dory was
so full by then that it was close to capsizing. "Naw, go away," they
yelled, "we're fine."

They drifted away from the freighter, were caught by the Gulf
Stream and carried north toward Fort Lauderdale. Their minuscule
motor was next to useless. They had to fight the sea for hours to
make landfall. J.R.'s voice on the tape radiates a huge good humor—
"This lifetime never had a hold of me like it did other people."

I wouldn't have put it the way J.R. did, but I knew exactly what
he meant. Risking my life on a whim—for the adrenaline kick, to
prove something, to prove nothing, just because I felt like it—was
something I did with scary regularity all through my teens and
well into my twenties. I can remember thinking, "If I get killed,
so what?"—or not thinking at all. I can remember lying in bed

for hours afterward, shaking with terror, and I can also remember feeling nothing despite the fact that I'd just come within an inch and a half of being as dead as a gaffed catfish. Maybe this lifetime didn't have much of a hold on me either—not at the beginning. Another way out, of course, was the old tried-and-true that both J.R. and I tried—drinking.

"By the 70s," J.R. says, "I was pretty much an alcoholic. I was out there lurking around, scrambling, trying to find my way again, and at that point . . . But then it all ended, everything ended right there for me . . . This is a long story."

"So tell me the story."

We all tried to outdrink each other in the service. When I got out, I hung out on the beach for a while, and then I moved inland to Miami Springs where the stewardesses were, and I loved to dance. You'd go to the clubs, and you'd dance all night, and you'd drink all night, and it was my sort of routine. In the airlines I got so much free booze off the airplanes, it was sort of a joke. I drank from the time that I left high school in '51 until the 70s, so I had a good run.

I was getting warnings. My body was falling apart, my face was looking like it got run over by a cement mixing truck. I loved to go waterskiing, and on one particular day a lot of people were going to show up at the house, and I was going to take them out. I probably slept two hours . . . got up, and I had the *worst* hangover. Without taking anything for it, I went out in the garage and started working on the outboard ski boat.

This is a story J.R. has told before, and he tells it with relish, pausing for effect in all the right places. It's designed to be both horrifying and funny—and it is. Mary and I are laughing at the first sign of disaster.

I had the whole unit up in the air with one hand, and it got away from me and tore off my left thumb. There was blood all over the place, and I passed out for a split second, went down on my knees. Obviously my thumb disappeared from view.

I went into the kitchen to wash off the blood, and that's when the full extent of the damage finally registered on me. There simply was no thumb. About half of it had been taken off.

One of my buddies turned up. I showed him what was left of my thumb, and *he* passed out.

So I got him up, but *I* had to drive *him* to the hospital in his car, and we get there, and I call an ex-roommate of mine who was a doctor. He was chief of staff of this small hospital. So he had his best friend, who was the top surgeon there, come in and take a look at me, and he cleaned off the thumb and everything, and was going to sew it up, and unbeknown to either one of us, this other friend of mine, this fireman, who I was going to take out waterskiing, came to the open garage and found there was a commotion from people across the street there. He said, "What happened to J.R.?"

They said, "He went to the hospital minus a thumb."

Bob didn't bat an eye. He looked around the garage, found the thumb in a bunch of oil and grease and blood, went in the kitchen, washed it off, wrapped it up, found out what hospital, and just made a beeline for it. He arrived at the moment that the surgeon was going to sew up my thumb and just—click—cap it. So he says in his four-letter-language, "Hey, motherfucker, what are you going to do with his thumb?"

He looks at it. I look at it. I say, "Is that really my thumb, Bob?"

He says, "Yeah." He says, "Hey, doc, what do you say we stick this thing back on?"

"Well, I don't think so."

"What do you mean?" I says. "If it doesn't grow, we'll take it back off."

The doctor's eyes go to the ceiling. So he prepares my stump. It was cut off down around here, and he stuck it on, sewed it up, knowing full well it wouldn't last. By that time, my ex-roommate, the doctor, shows up, and he takes a look. "Ah, J.R., what did you do? You've got to come in my office every day this week. I'm going to work on that thumb."

Whenever I went into his office, he took a long needle and pricked the top of the thumb to get blood to flow through it. I went in there every day for about two weeks, and the doctor did the same routine, and it took. There wasn't even a scar where that thumb had been sewed on.

But anyway, getting back to the thumb, I was sitting on the edge of the operating table, and I said, I'm going to make this *my thumb of knowledge*—that quaint little phrase. I got up one morning a couple weeks after that and looked in the mirror and saw a skull looking back at me. I said, this is very interesting. I said, that's old Father Death looking me in the face.

Since I was never fearful of death, I said, this is another warning, and I better take heed. It was literally on the spot that I decided to change my life.

As his old life ended, his new one began. "The turnaround was *so fast*," he says, like a man who still can't believe his own good luck. He stopped seeing his old buddies because they were a bunch of drunks and he didn't want to be around them anymore. He started going to psychic retreats. Everything he needed came to him the moment he needed it. A book would fall off the shelf and land open to exactly the page he should read. He'd walk into a room of strangers and find exactly the next person he should meet. One thing led to another, and the next fourteen years were the best of his life.

"What intrigued me," he says, "what has played out through my life . . . I'm interested in mysteries. My mother was an avid mystery reader. She had hundreds of those little pocketbooks lying around, and I got addicted to mysteries as a kid. So, as I looked at all the . . . the mystery of my life, the mystery of the family, and so, yeah, later on, I found out that life itself was a mystery. Forget all the characters in it, all the people in it, life itself is the grand mystery."

Yes, indeed, it is—especially for two mystified boys like us. We found out that the mystery has no solution, but in trying to solve it, we re-created ourselves. J.R. stepped into that stream of esoterica flowing out of the 60s that we call New Age spirituality. At times, I could almost be persuaded to his point of view—that everything is connected to everything else, that there are no accidents, that everything we do affects things on a higher plane, that things on that higher plane constantly affect us.

I, too, have psychic moments, but they always take me by surprise, and I don't build them into my worldview the way J.R. does. One afternoon I'd been thinking about him intensely for several hours and decided to call him up. I was reaching for the telephone when it rang. "What do you want?" he said, laughing.

I keep thinking about J.R.'s mother, that other lady who was so pissed off at Gene Maillard she wouldn't talk about him. Trying to read her from a distance, I'm just as puzzled by Ruth as J.R. was—"a very nice woman, but very private." I see her as a sad-eyed child hiding behind a series of consciously chosen adult masks. With her silences, lopsided attempts to imitate conversation, obsessive need for quiet and control, Ruth strikes me as someone who was working hard to impersonate a normal person. In the boozer, Peter Worden, she might have chosen a perfect mate—a man who would never notice anything the least bit odd about her. "By dinnertime," J.R. says, "my stepfather was always in the bag."

Peter told everyone that he would die at sixty-four—because his father, mother, and his first cousin had died at sixty-four. He stepped out of the bathroom one day, keeled over, and died. He was sixty-four. "As much as he drank," J.R. said, "every organ in his body must have been pickled."

After Peter died, Ruth packed up two suitcases and left them by the front door. J.R. asked her what she was doing. "Well," she said, "Peter is coming back to get me."

"That would be nice," J.R. said. "Yeah, and that's a good place to keep the suitcases."

He thought it would go on for a couple of days, but it went on for weeks. She left her suitcases there, fully packed, waiting for Peter to come back for her. Then one day when J.R. came to visit, he discovered that she'd taken all the wall plates off the walls. "Why did you do that?" he asked her. "Now all the wiring's exposed."

"We're being tested," she said. "This house is under surveillance, and the government is testing us. They're sending beams at us."

"Oh, okay, and by taking off the wall plates, what's that do?"

"Oh, it protects us . . . and by the way, they're really bombarding the roof. There's all kinds of metal up there, and you've got to go up there and get that metal off the roof."

J.R. went into the little shed at the back of the house and loaded himself up with nuts and bolts and old pieces of brass fixtures and anything metal. He got out the ladder and climbed up onto the roof. Ruth stood in the backyard with her arms crossed while J.R. pretended to find things. She had a little plastic bucket she used to take to the beach; when he'd throw something down, she'd put it in the bucket. J.R.'s decisive action must have foiled the government's sinister plot. Ruth never mentioned the magnetic bombardment again. She died a few years later.

13.

DEMENTIA GRADUALLY TOOK MY MOTHER away from me, and I grieved her passing years before she actually died. The horrifying thing about dementia is that you can't tell where the person has gone—or if there is anyone left at all. Although she became smaller, became frail, she didn't look terribly different from the mother I'd always known. For a while, she could fool me into thinking that she was still in the same land with the rest of us—could carry on a short conversation, say the automatic, polite things she'd said her whole life—but her memory span got shorter and shorter. By the end it was, the best I could tell, less than two minutes. For a while, she still possessed her childhood, could describe in detail the clothes she'd worn at six, but even that was taken away from her. She never lost the ability to speak, always knew who I was—who Mary and Jane and Elizabeth were—but eventually her response to any question was always the same: "Oh, Keith, I don't remember."

I remembered for her. Grieving, I remembered that apartment in Wheeling where she'd lived for nearly forty years. I'd walk up the narrow stairs, pass the black ceramic vase she'd made in high school—dried cat tails in it—pass the scroll I'd painted in high school—a Buddhist monk crossing a river, bringing the Dharma from India to China—and I'd smell the years of my mother's greasy cooking, hear the yap of her wretched little dog. I'd step into the living room and set my suitcase down. "Oh, honey," she'd say, "it's so good to see you," and there I'd be again in that little apartment looking out over Front Street where my grandmother had sat for so many years looking out at the river, where my mother would be sitting in front of the TV, and maybe later we'd drink beer and my mother would tell me again the stories I'd heard before—about dancing to Paul Whiteman above the Upper Market or about the time she'd organized the office staff at Interstate into the Teamsters' Union and how the company had promoted her to management so they could fire her.

When Liz was ten and Jane fifteen, my mother came to visit us. She insisted on bringing her dog with her. She's always owned small, yappy dogs—each one crazier than the last. "I needed something to love," she said. She hadn't bothered to toilet train Mitsie, so the damned dog shit and pissed on every rug in our house. Liz, who always liked animals, managed to extract Mitsie from my mother's lap once a day to take her outside—although it was a battle of the wills. My mother wanted to keep the dog glued to her like fly paper.

My mother was eighty-eight then. It was the last time I would have access to her memory while it was still reasonably intact, and I must have sensed it, because I gave her a carefully doled-out quantity of fine British Columbia microbrewery beer and got her talking into my tape recorder four straight days running. She talked about everything under the sun, but I kept guiding her back to Gene. By the time we were finished, I felt as though I'd squeezed every last possible drop of information out of her—or at least all that she was ever going to tell me.

The following year, when Liz and I went to visit my mother in Wheeling, she was already slipping over the divide into dementia. We kept finding scraps of dried-up dog food and lumps of petrified dog shit in corners and even behind the cushions of the fold-away bed. My mother was planning to leave Grandmother Sharp's small rocking chair to Liz and told her the story of it over and over again; she must have told her twenty times or more. "Doesn't she remember that she just told me?" Liz asked me.

"No," I said.

"I'm glad you brought me down here, Dad," Liz said. "I can see the person Granny used to be. She must've been a real nice person."

For years I had a fantasy that eventually my mother and I would sit down and talk to each other honestly, from the heart, and become, in some sense, reconciled, because there had always been a distance between us, and it had grown worse over the years. I imagined that we would have our perfect conversation when she was dying—imagined sitting by her bedside for several days as she departed in a leisurely manner, as we talked over everything and sorted it all out. I would walk away from her bedside feeling completed, and she would die knowing that we had reached a proper ending, that everything was all right between us. My fantasy was, of course, just that—a fantasy, and a fairly silly one at that—but then, a year after she had died, when I began to transcribe the tapes I'd made of her, I realized that we'd already had our perfect conversation. I worked through the tapes slowly, trying to preserve, in her honor, not merely the information she'd given me but the exact pattern of her speech, her particular Ohio Valley dialect.

While I'd been recording her, I'd been so deeply involved in the process that I hadn't fully realized what was happening. Of course I'd noticed that she was occasionally telling me things I'd never heard before, but it wasn't until I was actually listening to the tapes word for word—doing my best to preserve her every pause, her every um and ah—that I realized how significant some of those things were. Gene was a tap dancer, she told me matter-of-factly, but it was the first time she'd ever mentioned it.

"That snapshot of Gene standing with Bill and Uncle Will Brown . . ." I said, leading her.

"Do you have that picture?"

"Yeah. Mary actually had it enlarged. You know that picture?"

I brought the photo from the living room, set it down in front of her. She picked it up and studied it. "You know, after we were divorced, after I . . . Oh, yeah, I remember. After I left him, I tore everything up that had his picture on it."

I'd never heard her admit it before. "Well, you must have," I said, "because that's the only picture I've got."

"I did! I was so mad and so hurt, and I . . . Everything that had his picture on it, I tore it up. That's awful. But I was hurt."

She sat for a long time, holding the picture and looking at it. "Uncle Will and Gene . . ." She laughed. "And Bill."

"So how did Gene get along with the family? There he is with two of them."

"He was . . . He, he was . . . He was a good person, Keith. And a nice personality. Well liked. By everyone but me."

I knew that there was something more coming. "Oh, dear," she said eventually—and I could hear the sorrow and bewilderment in her voice—"I can't say anything against Gene Maillard. Other than the fact that I had this tie to Mother that I couldn't let go of. I knew what she had been through. I knew that every nickel she made, she sat up until midnight trying to get another stitch in something. She had a hell of a life when you get . . . but you'd never know it. She . . . Oh, I don't know."

"'It's a great life if you don't weaken,' she used to say."

"Yeah. That's right. That's right. I didn't know you had that picture."

"Do you think you would have done better if you hadn't gone off with Gene to Hot Springs? All of a sudden there you were in a completely unfamiliar place . . ."

"Well, the only reason that I moved out there with him was to try to save the marriage. I was so mad at him at that point that . . . I was hurt. When I got to Wheeling and got back on my feet, I went to see Charlie Ihlenfeld who was the prosecuting attorney. I'd gone to school with him and dated him, so I went to see him . . . and I said, 'He's not sending me any money.' He says, 'He will.' So he wrote to the prosecutor in Hot Springs. No! In Biloxi. Gene had left Hot Springs and gone to Biloxi. And Charlie wrote to the prosecutor down there, and I don't know what he said or anything else, but all I got was five dollars a week, but back then it was better than nothing. Oh, boy. I put all that behind me a long time ago. Why bring it up?"

She was still staring at the picture. "This amazes me, and pleases me. I didn't know that you had that. Gene wasn't a very big person. But he was quite a guy."

I was just as amazed as she was. That was the nicest thing I'd ever heard her say about my father.

Another part of the story I'd always known was that when she left Gene in Hot Springs, she went to stay with her sister and her husband. "I stayed at Martha's," she said, "not quite three weeks, and then she drove me to Wheeling. She and Harley were mighty good to me. That was quite an experience. So, after I was in Wheeling a while, I told Mother that if she would stay home and take care of you, I would go to work and keep her as long as she lived. So that was our arrangement . . . Give me another beer, and I'll tell you my life story."

We both laughed at that. "I haven't got another beer to give you."

"I know. That's the reason I said that . . . And that brings us up to Gene Maillard. He was a terrific guy, had a good sense of humor, but I didn't know him well enough when I married him, unfortunately . . . He was so tight he would take the paint off of a table if he could do it. Other than that, we got along great. There was nothing wrong with Gene. He was a good person, a good personality, and a lot of friends, but I couldn't stand that pinching pennies. And my family isn't like that, never has been."

"Well, he was a Depression kid from an immigrant background."

"That's right."

"He probably had to pinch every penny just to make it."

"That's right. Well, you see, Gene had a sister, Olga . . . whatever their name was. And she practically raised Gene. He was born in France, in Alsace-Lorraine, and that family migrated to Canada, someplace, Québec or someplace up there, and . . . ah . . . up *here*. I forget where I am. And . . . she sent Gene to a dance school because at that point men in musical comedy, and entertainers, you know, were all dancers. And she thought that was the way for Gene to go."

That was the standard story I'd always heard. I didn't see any point in trying to convince her that Gene had been born in Coraopolis, Pennsylvania. "Yeah, back in those days every movie had a tap dancer," I said.

"Yeah. Yeah. Bill Robertson, that black man. Fred Astaire. I can't name them all. But, ah . . . and he was good. But with all due respect to Gene Maillard, he was tighter than six hundred dollars. And still he died with money in the bank. How much I don't know, but the first dollar was in there, I'm sure. But I . . . I resented his attitude. He was the damn *tightest* . . . somebody. And then he dies and leaves all his money to . . ."

"The Masons."

"The Masons. Whatever. And by that point, he must have had plenty of it because he never spent it. So it was the Maillards against the Sharps. And you know the Sharps."

"Yeah. And Bill used to say, 'If you can't go first class, don't go.'"

"That's right, and I feel the same way. Oh, dear. That's another

. . . that's, that's the main thing that started Gene and my divorce. See, I was in Wheeling, and . . . When I had you, he wasn't there. So, of course, they wanted to know the name and everything, and they came in and wrote it all down, and I was in the hospital. And I said, "Keith Lee Maillard," so they wrote it down, and that's on your birth certificate. When Gene found out, he was furious. He had been the third Eugene Maillard, and he expected you to be the fourth. I said, 'Well, I don't give a damn what you think. He has a right to his own name.' Oh, dear. That was just the beginning. We found so many things. He thought I was extravagant as all hell . . . because I didn't save the milk off of the cereal to have it the next day. Oh, boy. Now that's tight."

"You're right. That *is* tight."

After a moment, I said, "I would have only been the third . . ."

"Hum?"

"I would have only been the third Eugene. His grandfather's name was Louis."

"Oh, you've looked it up?"

"Yeah, I have."

"Well, anyhow."

Anyone listening to the playback at that point would probably suspect that the interview had ended and I'd forgotten to turn off the tape recorder. Several minutes went by as my mother looked at me and I looked at her.

She stood up and addressed her dog. "Come on, baby. I have to go change my shoes."

14.

MY MOTHER HAD SUMMONED HER DOG, changed her shoes, and walked off into eternity leaving me with the same puzzling task I'd always had—trying to read her mind from her silence. "You've been looking up your father's family?" I imagined her thinking. "Well, then, I'm not going to tell you another damned thing." I was sure that she'd already told me far more than she'd intended, and that was the end of it.

She was gone, but I still had the tape. By the time I'd finished transcribing it, I'd come smack up against something so obvious that I should have seen it years ago. My grandmother hadn't been merely a bit player in my parents' break-up—she'd been at the center of it.

Some girls are lucky enough to look exactly right for the style of their generation, and Mabel Thomas was one of them. In her early photographs, she's the perfect Gibson Girl—immaculate in long white dresses, her hair piled up on the back of her head, blessed with the handsome, vigorous, self-assured face that was admired then. She also had the upright, ramrod posture that girls were supposed to have—and often did, laced as they were into the long straight-front corsets of the day. She'd been proud of her waistline. After Addison was born, her family doctor said, "Mamie, you're never going to have an eighteen-inch waist again." She didn't think that was fair. I never heard her complain about anything, but she did have differences with God. When, in her eighties, she fell off a stepladder and broke her hip—she'd been washing the walls—she told me that she didn't like it that human beings are made to grow old. "If I'd been doing it," she told me, "I wouldn't have designed the world that way."

She told me that her one big regret was marrying young. She'd always wanted to be a nurse—to her that meant independence and respect—but at nineteen, she married Philo Adam Sharp, had her first baby ten months later, and then had three more, timed neatly two years apart.

Obsessed as they were with clothes, with style, with looking *just right*, P.A. Sharp and Mabel Thomas must have made a handsome couple. In the early years of their marriage, when, as my grandmother put it, "P.A. was young and in love," he sent her a dozen pink carnations every Valentine's Day. He was only a year older than she was, so he would have been twenty when he decided to strike out on his own and secured a first-rate position in Chicago. "Dad was a terrific shoe salesman," my mother told me. "He knew shoes from the ground up." But he knew cards too—or he thought he did—and the money from shoes vanished into that fabulous and endless poker game that would engage his considerable intellect for the rest of his life. Broke and by then a father, P.A. removed to Pittsburgh to have another go at it.

"Jack of Diamonds, Jack of Diamonds, I know you of old . . ." my mind sings as I write this—another shoe store, but the same old song. When stripped down to nothing and hung out to dry, P.A. did what he always did—came back to the Valley and sponged off his dad. Zerah Sharp, retired from the haberdashery business, would eventually have no savings left because he would have given it all to P.A.

After yet a second disaster in Pittsburgh, my grandmother decided she "couldn't live like that." She left P.A., came home, dumped Addison, Martha, and Bill with relatives—various obscure aunts and uncles I still can't keep straight in my mind—and, hanging onto my mother, the baby, moved back in with her parents in Kirkwood, Ohio. Here enters into the drama a major player—my la-dee-dah Aunt Clara. She never forgave Mabel for marrying P.A. The Sharps were so superior to the Thomases in every way that even a headstrong girl like Mabel Thomas should have known better.

Clara Sharp had done what girls were supposed to do—married well—first to a Belgian businessman and then to a wealthy Wheeling doctor, so she was in a position to help out her charming and brilliant younger brother who was sure to make his mark one day soon. It was not right that P.A.'s kids were scattered all over the place—they were *Sharps*, after all. Clara made a deal with my grandmother: "You get your family, your children, back together, and I'll pay your rent," and she paid it for years while P.A. played cards and contributed nothing. Mabel would have had very little choice in the matter. Women had just begun to enter the work force, but even if she could have found a job, it wouldn't have paid enough for her to support four kids. "I'll see all the children through high school," Clara told her. It must have galled Mabel down to the bone to be dependent on Clara Sharp.

"They were just like two roosters," my mother told me. "Mother and Clara. Neither one of them would condescend enough even to look at the other one."

Mabel wanted her kids educated in the big, bustling city of Wheeling, so she crossed the river into West Virginia and rented a house on the Island. Talking about changing his ways, about new beginnings, P.A. rejoined his wife and family. Then one weekend there occurred the last fatal poker game. Who knows why that game was different from any of the previous games, but for my grandmother it was one game over the line. She had the locksmith change the locks on the doors. She locked P.A. out of the house, and never let him back in. Clara lived up to her promise and continued to pay the rent, but my grandmother never spoke to her again, and she never spoke to P.A. again, not once, for as long as she lived.

We've all done it—worked our way in and out of a love affair or a marriage. However much of a mess it was, however much it changed the entire course of our life, we have the sense of having been involved in the process, of having decided one way or another. We might end up scarred, but at least we can take responsibility for some of the shit that went down. The sudden tragedy that comes out of nowhere is a different story. As horrific as the breakup of my grandmother's marriage undoubtedly was, the death of her younger sister—earlier, in 1918—must have been worse.

My grandmother assessed everyone, even those she loved. Bill was "weak," Addison "opinionated," and so on through the whole family to arrive at "dreamy" me. There were only two people she seemed to have loved without qualifiers—her easy-going dad, the riverboat captain, and her younger sister, Eva. "She was a wonderful person," she told me. "She had such a sunny disposition. Every day was a new day to Eva." I heard the story of Eva's death many times from my grandmother, but I don't have her words, and I do have my mother's—preserved on that same tape. The "Wilson" in the story is Eva's little son.

> Everybody adored Eva. She was the pet of Kirkwood. She'd bake cookies, she'd bake bread, she'd fix a meal to the poorest family on the hill and carry it in a basket up. . . you know, to feed the family. She was a terrific person, and a . . . It was the Fourth of July. Wilson and I were playing on the back porch of Bennett

Street. Eva was in the house, getting dinner, and she was fixing all this stuff, you know, for a picnic, and . . . She had long hair, but it was all in a bun in the back, and in some way—I never did understand how—her hair caught on fire. And she went this way, which took it all down out of the pin, and ran out the back door with her hair hanging down in flames.

And this . . . Hoover. Mr. Hoover was sitting on his back porch up across this alley, and when she ran out screaming, he ran down, through the alley, and jumped. It was like a wall. And grabbed a rag rug off of the line and just threw it over her and wrapped her in it and rolled her on the ground. That's the only thing that saved her life. But . . . See, then they didn't take them to the hospital. The doctors came to the house. So, by the time that . . . Oh, can't think of his name. Who did Eva marry? Wilson's father? George Connelly.

It *was* George. Ah . . . I get sidetracked. By the time they got in touch with George, she was out of her mind, you know. It was just a shock, and this man down the street—I don't remember who that was—came up. Everybody in Kirkwood came. You know, it was one of these things that everybody yelled so-and-so, and Eva was so well known and liked, and this man says, "Draw the bathtub full of water," and he sat in that bathroom with his hand on the edge of the tub with her chin in his hand and kept her head . . . kept her submerged in water until the doctor got there, and . . . Mary Frankhauser, she was the big nurse, heard about it, and she quit. She had a patient somewhere. She says, "I'm sorry. I have to quit," and she came over, and her directions . . . She said, "put big hooks up in the ceiling, and get me wide canvas strips." And they hung these strips and lined it with cotton, and put Eva—I can still see her—on the strips. And they just kept moving them all the time. She couldn't stand to . . . Her flesh was just burned off. And they kept moving them to ease her.

They didn't have the drugs they have today. But, oh . . . That was on the Fourth of July, and she died on Thanksgiving. And the reason she died . . . That was the flu epidemic. Everybody in Kirkwood had it. Couldn't get my head off the pillow, none of us could. Even Mother had it that bad, and Dad's the one that had to take care of the whole bunch. He never got it. And he took care of all of us. Mother, and . . . The neighbors would come with big baskets of food and put it on the porch and run. They didn't want to have anything at all to do with us. We were quarantined. Great big red sign on the front of your house. It said, "Quarantine. Stay out." They were afraid that if Eva got the flu, it'd kill her—which it did. It was George brought it to her.

George was working at Klevis Lumber Company as a clerk, and one night he went in to see Eva, of course, and kissed her and talked to her, and spent the evening with her, and she got the flu and died. She was on the mend. She was . . . Wilson and I would stand in the door, and they had her bandaged, and all you could see was the tips of her fingers, and her eyes, and she would go like this with her fingers to us.

I saw her when she caught fire. She ran past us. Wilson and I were on the porch, but it was so fast, Keith, it didn't register what was happening. We were just . . . I was six. Wilson was five. I still see . . . Oh, Mr. Hoover. Coming down off of this wall down there, and grabbing the rag rug, and throwing it . . . and by that time, someone got Wilson and me by the hand, and we were gone. That's all I remember about that.

Oh, Lord, by that time, there were a hundred people around. See, in my mind I can still see Mr. Hoover coming down, and . . . He was a streetcar motorman. He was a pretty big person. But that too is vague. I don't know what she caught her hair on. I don't know. She was at the stove. I don't know how it caught. But then she ran, the . . . all this hair . . . and she had beautiful blond hair, long. Of course back in those days, they didn't cut their hair. And when she ran, all this hair was behind her, burning.

She was only in her twenties. She had the biggest funeral that Kirkwood had ever seen at that point. They lived in the second house from the corner, and the people standing in line to come in there . . . This I remember! . . . You could look down the street, and they were still down there, turning, down the street, there was that many people. They just came. Black and white. They didn't stop. They just came through the house, and out the back door . . . to see Eva. She was a person if anybody was sick—it didn't make any difference who they were—she would fix them a meal. She had the . . . In fact, I still have the basket. The basket with a lid on it? Do you remember that? That was Eva's basket that she took food to these people. And in Kirkwood everybody knew everybody else, and . . . Oh, the people. I can still see this. Of course they had her at home, in the living room, and the casket was catty-cornered across the corner down there, and people would come in, and those women would just cry and cry . . . because she was an angel to them. No one ever went hungry that she ever heard about. Black or white. In the back of my mind, I can see her as a blonde with her hair done high. That's my memory of Eva.

My grandmother was thirty-one when Eva was burned. She too saw it happen right before her eyes. In her account, there were a number of men who sat, frozen and indecisive, and watched. They were much closer to Eva than Mr. Hoover who had to jump a wall to get to her. One of those men who sat and watched—who did nothing—was my grandfather, P.A.

I see Eva's death chopping my grandmother's life in half as cleanly and savagely as a meat cleaver chops a melon. For months afterward, my grandmother was partially paralyzed on her left side.

At the time they called it nerve paralysis. Now we might diagnose it as post-traumatic stress disorder. "The paralysis went away," my mother told me, "but she never got over it."

If I draw the line of that terrible year—1918—across the lives of Mabel Sharp's four kids, I see it as dividing them into those who got away and those who didn't. Martha was ten and Addison twelve, both old enough to resist and pull free. They grew up, married, and left town.

But my mother, Aileen, was six, my uncle Bill eight, and I'm guessing that my grandmother drew them to her—to protect them and keep them safe—*and never let go.*

"Mother babied Bill something awful," my mother told me. Bill wasn't the only one who was babied something awful. If Mary and I could see it in pictures, my grandmother would have seen it every day in the flesh—how much my mother looked like Eva Thomas.

Aileen was the youngest, the smallest, the cutest—the blonde. By the time she graduated from high school, she was as tall as she was ever going to get—four-foot eleven—a little fashion plate, by her own lights "the best dressed girl at Wheeling High." At eighteen, she still thought a girl could get pregnant from a kiss. At twenty, although she was working by then, making her own money and proud of it, she was not allowed out alone at night. No boy she dated would ever come up to my grandmother's high standard. When my mother fell deeply in love with the boy she *should* have married—that's what she always said about him—my grandmother broke them up. I know nothing about the boy who got away except his flamboyant name—Royal Sims—but he was still on my mother's mind in her eighties.

When, on the rebound, my mother married Gene Maillard, she did it against her mother's wishes. When Gene took her to Hot Springs, Arkansas, she would have been, for the first time in her life, entirely on her own.

15.

EVER SINCE GENE'S SCRAPBOOKS had first appeared in our lives, Mary had been searching for my father's family. It wasn't yet a full-time project for her, just something she did in her spare time. I tried to sound interested, but I didn't really care. My mind was elsewhere. "Where the hell is Follansbee, West Virginia?" she asked me one afternoon.

Her question came out of nowhere, and I couldn't imagine why she was asking. "You don't remember?" I said. "We've driven through there. It's up the River Road from Wheeling, right next to Wellsburg."

Mary had been searching for my father's family in Montréal. They were French, so obviously they must be Catholic—that's what we'd always thought—but she'd found my great-grandfather, old Louis Maillard, the patriarch, buried in Mount Royal Cemetery. The date was right—1909—but why was he in the *Protestant* cemetery?

She'd called the cemetery office in Montréal. The records revealed no more information about Louis than what we already knew, but two other people were buried with him. One of them was his daughter, Eugenie. Her last place of residence was *Follansbee, West Virginia.*

It didn't make any sense. Mary's search shouldn't be leading us back to West Virginia—that's where we'd started. We stared at each other, spooked, sharing again that too-weird-for-words feeling—the great snake of the world looping around to bite its own tail. And how could old Louis have named a son Eugene and a daughter *Eugenie*? That name must have had enormous totemic significance for the Maillards.

Eugenie's next of kin was someone named Emil Brunet in Follansbee, West Virginia. There was an Emil Brunet in the US phone directory—*in Follansbee, West Virginia*. "That's got to be Emil's son," Mary said and called the number.

No, it wasn't Emil Brunet's son. It was his elderly widow. "That's right," she said, "Eugenie was my mother-in-law. We took her body back to Montréal to bury her with her father. That's right, it would have been 1952. I was on the train with her. Oh, yes, the Maillards were Protestants. They were all Presbyterians."

Oh, my God, I thought, I'm a Huguenot.

After months of going nowhere, following a dozen false leads, we had arrived at a dizzying breakthrough. In a matter of days we'd gone from having next to no information to being inundated with it, and now I was just as fascinated as Mary was. A big chunk of the Maillard family had moved from Montréal to West Virginia in the teens. My grandfather, Eugene F., was buried in the Brooke County Cemetery in Wellsburg—and, incredibly, so was his mother, my great-grandmother, Marie Louise Paillet Maillard. We hadn't been able to find them because West Virginia hadn't begun to keep death records until 1923.

When I'd been wondering why I was a brown-eyed kid in a blue-eyed family, my brown-eyed relatives had been living right up the river in West Virginia. When I'd pinned the Canadian flag to my wall, when I'd tried to learn French from a record, when I'd imagined myself as the fourth Eugene—a boy in a beret, carrying a baguette—my French relatives from Montréal had been living right up the river. In those years when it would have meant something enormous and shining to me, they'd been there all along. You can drive from Wheeling to Follansbee in half an hour. It was too big. I didn't know what to do with it.

I took Gene's scrapbooks out of their storage box, laid them on my desk, and turned their pages again. I'd been through them dozens of times, but there was still something that was eluding me. Gene had used them to construct a public image of himself; he was saying, "This is who I am"—the entertainer, the teacher, the Mason, the successful man, the philanthropist—but there was no narrative attached, no explanation of why he'd pasted one thing next to another.

Looking for a pattern, I catalogued everything in the scrapbooks. By the time I was finished, I knew what was in them— and, just as significantly, I knew *what was not*. When Gene had said that he'd disowned his family, he'd meant it. He hadn't documented his family, he'd documented *himself*. His father, mother, and paternal grandparents appeared on the first page of the black scrapbook, and that was pretty much all there was of his family until his sister, Olga, appeared as a middle-aged woman late in the brown scrapbook.

The other obvious hole was Gene's adolescence. He'd included a professional photographer's shot of him dancing on stage when he was nine or ten, but he'd pasted in nothing after that until he was a young man in his twenties. That didn't feel right to me— not for the obsessive collector of memorabilia he'd been. He'd left no evidence behind—not even a high-school class picture, not the smallest clue as to where he'd lived or what had happened to his parents or his numerous half-siblings. Maybe he'd stored his teenage keepsakes in a box that had been thrown away by mistake, or maybe they'd been destroyed in a natural disaster, like a fire— but no, I didn't believe that. When Gene had told the tale of his unhappy childhood to Kippy, he'd opened by saying, "My father died young." For most of us, our teenage years are nothing if not *memorable*, but Gene must not have wanted to remember his. I guessed that his adolescence must have been profoundly unhappy.

Mary is a documentary editor. She does not collect memorabilia; she collects information. She doesn't make scrapbooks; she stuffs file folders full of documents, and she writes footnotes. Since she'd found my relatives in Follansbee, she'd been going full speed ahead. There were obviously a lot more Maillard relatives floating around out there somewhere, and, by God, she was going to find every single one of them.

Everybody leaves a record. Whenever one of my relatives was born, when they were married or buried—when they sailed to or from Europe—when they crossed the border between the United States and Canada—when they applied for citizenship or a social security number or signed up for the draft—some official noted it down. Every few years a census taker came around and asked them questions. Occasionally they got themselves written up in newspapers. Mary could access all of those records.

She wasn't finding just dead relatives but living ones too—my second cousins in West Virginia, Pennsylvania, Ontario, Alberta, and, to our surprise, *first* cousins in British Columbia. One of them, a sparkly lady in her late eighties, living just a couple hours away, turned out to be another Eugenie; she had grown up called by the same name as my father—*Gene Maillard*. I talked to my new-found relatives on the phone, exchanged emails with them, met and interviewed some of them. They sent me photographs and clippings. Another Canadian cousin sent me copies of letters from

Louis and Eddie Maillard—Gene's two older half-brothers, the
ones who'd played in bands. Primary source material like that was
pure gold. I could hear the distinctive voices of my uncles sounding
in their written words.

As the years passed, Mary's file boxes filled up the closet in her
office, then took up half of the closet in mine. Eventually they
began to pile up on the floor in front of my bookcase. It was Mary's
job to collect that stuff, my job to figure out what to do with it.
I was faced with the same problem that faces a historian—I was
going to have to decide what to select from that massive amount
of material, decide what pattern to make of it.

It took the Maillards awhile to get to West Virginia. The Maillard
men were glassblowers, and glassblowers were nomads. To follow
their movement through the world was to follow the fortunes
of glass plants. My grandfather, Eugene F., was born in France,
learned his craft in Montréal, and then moved from there to
Indiana, to Georgia, to Ontario. Back in Montréal, he married
a French-Canadian girl—Elisa Vallee, the daughter of a glassblower—and fathered his first son, Edouard. Still following the
work, he returned to Indiana where his second son, Louis, was
born—and where his young wife died, probably from complica-
tions of childbirth.

The motherless boys, Eddie and Louis, were raised in Montréal
by their Maillard grandparents while Eugene F. traveled back
and forth across the border to work, sending his money home to
his family. Blowing glass in Coraopolis, Pennsylvania, Eugene F.
met and married his second wife, my grandmother, Clementine.
With her and her children—and his new infant son, my father—
he moved yet again, to work for McBeth-Evans in Charleroi,
Pennsylvania.

Gene's childhood memories would have been, like mine, of a town with a river running by it—in his case, the Monongahela—of a large complex family, thickly interconnected with shared histories. Like me trying to sort through my extended family, Gene would have been wondering, who are these people—who's related to me *by blood*? Of the kids crammed into Eugene F.'s household, Gene would have been the only one of them related to *everybody* by blood. His mother's children—John Tommasini, Frank and Olga Serpagli—were his half-siblings; so were his father's children, Eddie and Louis, the boys from Montréal. The Mariani kids living just a few houses up the street were Gene's cousins from his mother's side of the family.

The first family story Gene would have heard must surely have been about his own name. "You were named to honor your great-grandfather," Gene's Papa would have told him. "His name was like yours—just turned around. He was Charles Eugene Maillard. I am named to honor him too—and so is your Tante Eugenie. You are the third son named Eugene."

The first Eugene was a glassblower, as was his father before him, and his father's father before that—*tel père, tel fils*—as far back as anyone could remember. Surely Gene was supposed to become a glassblower too.

As more family stories were passed on to him, Gene would have heard them in French and remembered them in French. Old Louis, Gene's grandfather, had fought in the Franco-Prussian War—and the French had lost it. The border had been moved, putting the Maillard's home behind enemy lines. The Germans had seized a small chunk of French territory and glued it together with an entirely different region to create a bogus entity they called "Alsace-Lorraine." Before 1871, Alsace-Lorraine had never existed; after 1918, it would never exist again, but when Gene heard the story, that's the name that was used, and that's what he would tell my mother, who would tell me: "The Maillards came from Alsace-Lorraine."

No, they didn't. Alsace-Lorraine is a German fiction. The Maillards came from Lorraine—from the village of Allamps.

In the fourteenth century, Duke John I had invited glassmakers to come and settle in Lorraine, and glass has been blown there ever since. Allamps is forty miles from Bacarat, famous for what many consider to be the finest flint crystal in the world.

Since we'd first seen Gene's scrapbooks, we'd known about old Louis Maillard who "played tuba and directed military bands in Montréal," but now we could identify the other people who appeared in Gene's various accounts of himself. The "twin aunts who played piano" were Tante Louise and Tante Emilie, two of Louis's three daughters; as old women, they resembled each other so much that it's impossible to distinguish them in photographs, and Gene could well have taken them for twins. "The older brothers who organized a band"—Eddie and Louis—were key players in Gene's early life. They're the ones who'd spent their childhoods in that musical household in Montréal. Except for what was in his blood, Gene's immediate musical legacy must have passed to him though Eddie and Louis.

The French boys from Montréal would have arrived in Charleroi with not much English but would have been young enough to pick it up in a flash—on the playgrounds and baseball diamonds, in the streets. As grown men, they would speak American English without a trace of an accent. They "became professional musicians in separate bands," Gene's interview with the *Columbia Basin News* tells us. If "professional" means getting paid, then Eddie and Louie might be called professional musicians, but Eugene F. had brought them down to Charleroi to learn the craft of glassblowing at McBeth-Evans, and learn it they did. They were professional glassblowers who played music in their spare time.

By the time Gene told his story again to the *Times-Advocate* in Escondido, it had become more concise:

> Maillard began to dance while just a tot in Pennsylvania. His older brothers organized a band, and young Gene kicked up his heels when they played.
>
> "I turned out to be a ham," he said. "I just got up and performed."

How old is "just a tot"? If we make Gene five, then Eddie is fourteen and Louis thirteen. Just the way that kids with music in their bones have always done it—are still doing it—the boys from Montréal must have slapped together a band as soon as they could. What was it like? We might be hearing some of ragtime's stiff syncopations, but we're years away from jazz—so far back in time that "Wait till the Sun Shines, Nellie" is a brand-new tune. There's no drummer yet, no tuba or bass player or banjo player, but the boys are playing dance music, and the percussion has to come from somewhere, so it probably comes from the piano, the chords pounded out hard and square so that the dancers will never have to worry about the beat. There's surely a fiddle or two and maybe a button-box accordion straight from the old country. These are French kids playing for French people, and if we could hear them, they would probably sound to us like an old-time ethnic band.

What instruments did they play? With Eddie, we know the answer. His family would remember him as a natural-born musician—a sonic wizard who didn't have to worry too much about the dots on the paper because he could pick up a tune as

soon as he heard it. For most of his life, Eddie formed and led
dance bands. Thanks to his aunts in Montréal, he could play the
piano—churning out music by the yard for silent movies—but
that was entirely by ear and he didn't take it seriously. His main
instrument, the love of his life, was the slick, sleek, all-purpose,
up-to-date, golden horn—the saxophone.

Louis is another matter. No one would remember him playing
any instrument at all, but my information comes from people
who called him "Uncle Louis," and the first story I heard was very
much from a child's point of view—at family gatherings, instead
of hanging out with the grown-ups, he'd get down on the floor and
play "snakes and ladders" with the kids. Oh yes, he was musical,
they assured me. He was a man who loved to sing.

Maybe when the Great War interrupted his life—he served
as an interpreter for the US army in France—Louis laid down a
trumpet or a clarinet and never picked it up again, but it's more
likely that no one remembered his instrument because it wasn't
something he could have carried around. If Eddie learned just
enough piano to blow it off, Louis might have actually paid
attention to his aunts and become good at it. So maybe it was
Louis who was laying down those solid chords for the dancers.

In the scene I'm imagining, Eddie and Louis are trying out their
pick-up band on family and friends in someone's home. This is not
a real job with money attached—the real jobs will come later—but
the house is packed, and everyone's dancing. I see Eddie pretending
to be a band leader, learning how to play that role. When he's not
blowing his sax, he leans against the wall in a picturesque slouch
that the younger boys are already beginning to emulate. With his
workman's cap and to-hell-with-you grin, Eddie could be acting
out the words of the song—"There may be flies on the rest of you
guys, but there ain't no flies on me."

Five-year-old Gene might be in the midst of one of those

magical childhood nights that shine in our memories forever. Of
course his parents are there—he would have called them "Papa"
and "Maman"—Eugene F. and Clementine. Let's imagine them
dancing, laughing, drinking a little homemade wine. Gene's half-
sister, Olga Serpagli, is ten and has a starring role in Gene's life.
She's the only girl in the Maillard household, and her mother does
to her what moms have always done to their daughters; whether
the message comes in French, Italian, or English, it's always the
same—"Olga! Watch out for your little brother, will ya?"

Clementine's eldest son, John Tommasini, is seventeen, already
a grown man working as a pipe-fitter at the glassworks, so he's
probably somewhere else, courting the local girl he'll later marry.
Thirteen-year-old Frank Serpagli, Clementine's second son, is
the rotten half-brother who tormented Gene as a child—I'll get
to that story later—and I don't feel like writing him into this
picture, so I'll send him off to the streets to hang out with a pack
of wisecracking boys out of a Booth Tarkington novel.

Charleroi, Pennsylvania, was planned around a glassworks and
named for its sister town in Belgium, famous for its glassworks.
As the industry dries up in Europe, more and more Belgian
glassblowers are coming to Charleroi in America. There are so
many French speakers in Charleroi that not only is there a French
Catholic church but even a French *Presbyterian* one; if the
Maillards are church-going people, that's where they go. Eddie
and Louis and all the young people would be speaking English to
each other—they're *Americans* after all—and the boys would be
playing all the American tunes they know, the hit tunes of their
day—the old chestnuts from "Bill Bailey" to "Ta-Ra-Ra-Boom-
De-Ay," the songs my grandmother sang with me as we danced
around the kitchen, "Daisy, Daisy" and "Waltz Me around Again
Willie." But they also would be playing enough French tunes
to keep the old folks happy. Surely somebody will sing, "*Plasir*

d'amour ne dure au'un moment. Chagrin d'amour dure toute la vie." Sigh.

After a slow soppy song like that, they take it up tempo. "*Les musiciens font comme ça,*" and that's Eddie's cue to clamp down on his mouthpiece and blow the tune out the other end—to decorate it like a wedding cake. Here comes the verse that Eddie adores— "*Les jeunes filles font comme ça.*" Ah, the *jeunes filles*—it's their cue to flirt, to tease the boys, to tease *him*—so he can grin them down. *Les jeunes filles* will be Eddie's delight his whole life long.

Look at that kid jumping up and down in front of the band. "He's so funny," the girls are squealing. "Say, Gene," Eddie yells, "what do you want, you little squirt? You want to play with the band? You, Olga! Give that kid something to bang on."

Gene's big sister fetches a pot from the kitchen, gives it to Gene, and a wooden spoon. Laughing, Gene bangs out the beat, jumping up and down like a wind-up toy—and there's my father's first appearance in the world as a dancer and a percussionist.

One tune that Eddie and Louis could certainly have played was "In the Baggage Coach Ahead." It was a smash hit in 1896, and the sheet music for it would have been everywhere.

"Listen, squirt," I imagine Eddie saying to Gene, "here's the song about Papa and Louis. I'm not in the song, but I was there too."

> On a dark stormy night, as the train rattled on,
> All the passengers had gone to bed,
> Except one young man with a babe in his arms
> Who sat there with a bowed-down head.
>
> The innocent one began crying just then,
> As though its poor heart would break.
> One angry man said, "Make that child stop its noise,
> For it's keeping all of us awake."

"Put it out," said another, "Don't keep it in here
Since we've paid for our berths and want rest."
But never a word said the man with the child,
As he fondled it close to his breast.

"Where is its mother? Go take it to her,"
This a lady then softly said.
"I wish I could," was the man's sad reply.
"But she's dead in the coach ahead."

Eugene F.'s first wife, Elisa Vallee, died in 1894 in Alexandria, Indiana. According to a legend preserved by her French-Canadian family, "In the Baggage Coach Ahead" told the story of her final journey back to Montréal for burial. The song was written by Gussie Lord Davis—we remember him now as the composer of "Goodnight, Irene"—and published in 1896. As the Vallees tell the story, Davis had been a porter on a Pullman car and witnessed the incident. Whether Gene heard it from his brothers or not, he would have known that song. When he wrote his own songs years later, he would strike much the same old sentimental chord.

In a portrait taken in Montréal the year before my father was born, we can see old Louis Maillard surrounded by his family—wife, son, three daughters, and two grandsons—all of them turned out in their best formal attire. Eugene F. would have been home on a visit; he was blowing glass in Coraopolis, Pennsylvania, where he would have already met my grandmother. None of the girls—Louise, Emilie, or Eugenie—was married yet, so they would have been still living with their parents and must have seemed more like big sisters to Eddie and Louis than aunts. The little boys would have spoken no other language but French, and this warm, respectable, musical household would have been the only home they had ever known.

Eddie and Louis are dressed identically in knickers and jackets with enormous white sailor-style collars flowing over their shoulders, sitting on stools in front of their grandfather, their hands resting lightly on his knees with an air of long familiarity. By the time we were given this picture, Mary and I had already identified a certain set of features we called "the Maillard look." Louis, six years old, has it in spades. On the face of a child, it's a melancholy look. If you study photographs of me, my father, J.R., and my uncle Louis, all of us at the age of six, you see that melancholy. Here, dark-eyed Louis is regarding us with a sad, shy, questioning, slightly mistrustful gaze that seems to be saying, "Is everything all right?"

Eddie is eight. He looks entirely different from the people around him. He's got the brilliant blue eyes, powerful jaw, and broad nose of his mother's people, the Vallees. There's not a drop of melancholy in him. They've managed to settle him down long enough to get the picture taken, but he's clearly ready to leap up at a moment's notice and run off. His face is self-assured and cocky. I read his expression as saying, "Yeah? So what?"

The boys we see in this photograph have already assumed the roles they will play for the rest of their lives. Louis, the shy boy, the nice boy, will grow up to be kind, soft-spoken, responsible Uncle Louis who cared for an ailing wife. Joseph Edouard will grow up to be Fast Eddie Maillard.

16.

NOW'S THE TIME FOR GENE'S STORY of child abuse—the older half-brother and cousin who tormented him as a kid. The brother was Frank Serpagli, the cousin Angelo Mariani Junior. As Gene told it, "When I came home from school, they were watching me from the upstairs window." That makes Gene at least six. Frank would have been fourteen, Angelo thirteen.

Gene walks upstairs. The boys grab him and chuck him out the window. Gene—light, small, and agile as a cat—splats into the muddy rain-soaked front lawn, breaks his fall with his knees and elbows. Bruised, the wind knocked out of him, stunned and scared, he hears the boys hooting two floors up. If they could do the unthinkable, if they could do *that*, what else could they do? What else *had they already done*? I ask myself now.

Gene's other story is so strange and repellent that I have to imagine exactly the right details, and enough of them, to make myself believe it. They heated a metal bar in a fire and made him carry it. How on earth could you even dream up something like that? My own childhood gives me a clue—from a movie about Robin Hood. I sat in the theater, sickened but unable to look away, as the minions of evil King John forced a peasant to undergo an ordeal to prove his testimony. They heated a metal bar in a fire and made him carry it. Frank could have read the same story.

This is not an angry boy's spontaneous violence. It takes a certain twist of mind—cold, detached, and instinctively cruel—to be attracted to a scheme like this, to put it into action. Frank Serpagli was one messed-up kid.

Frank must have bided his time. He had to wait until everyone was out of the house, the boys at work, his mother and his sister visiting somewhere—maybe at the Marianis—and not likely to come home very soon. There were two fires he could have used—the coal-burning furnace in the basement or the wood-burning stove in the kitchen. In order for the trial to work, the bar had to be just right—cool enough so Gene could carry it a few steps but hot enough to burn him good. Frank tests the temperature with his thumb.

"Hey, Frank, I don't know," I imagine Angelo saying, a whine in his voice. He's the younger sidekick, the follower. He's always gone along with Frank before, but this one doesn't feel right. He'd thought they were just going to scare the crap out of the kid.

Frank doesn't even look at Angelo. He's attending to Gene. "Pick it up and carry it," he says. "Show us you're a man. You just have to carry it over *there*."

Frank leans closer, smiling. "If you do it, we'll let you alone. We'll never pick on you again, swear to God Almighty. All you have to do is carry it. Come on, Gene, *pick it up*."

Gene's got sand in his craw, and he knows it. He's got grit and determination. He *is* a man, and he'll show them. He hauls in his breath and seizes the bar.

Shock smears red, the world in smithereens, but he's got it. Hasn't dropped it yet. Screws himself down like a spring, takes a step. Then another. CLUNG—the bar rings on the floor. Lost, Gene howls like a dog.

Frank grabs Gene by his hair, jerks his head up. "You tell and I'll cut your throat." For the rest of his life, Gene's nightmares will wear Frank Serpagli's face.

Clementine is no fool. "It was an accident"—that's all Gene will say. Every morning and every night she wets her youngest son's hands with buttermilk and wraps them in clean cotton. Accident? Are you kidding? You can't piss on my ass and tell me it's rain.

My grandmother was born as Clementina Mariani in Compiano, Parma, Italy, but she'd spent her childhood in a convent school near Paris. She spoke Italian, several dialects of it, but she also spoke French like a native, changed her name to Clementine, and thought of herself as French—so much so that when Gene would enter her birthplace into my mother's family tree, he would write, "Parma, *France*." When she'd been fourteen, her brothers—Angelo and Joseph—had sprung her from the convent and brought her to the new country to join their eldest brother in Pittsburgh. Just as my cousin Frank Wade had told me, Clementine had been married three times but not exactly to the men he'd listed. At sixteen she'd married Peter Luccidi, a tailor; their marriage did not last long, and Luccidi's name seems to have been lost to the family memory. We can find no evidence that she was ever married to John Tommasini's father; she did, however, just as everyone in the family remembered, marry Ludovico Serpagli—although not until several months after Frank was born—and then, finally, my grandfather. She filed for divorce from both Luccidi and Serpagli on the same grounds—desertion and nonsupport.

In twelve years she's had three sons by three different men, and she has also been a mother to her husband's sons from Montréal, so now she knows a thing or two about boys. Francesco was behind Gene's "accident"—that's as clear to her as if he'd signed his name on Gene's hands. She could swear sometimes the devil himself lived inside that boy. The person to talk to, of course, is her brother Angelo Mariani—Angelo Junior's father. "I don't know what you're going to do with young Angelo," I imagine her saying to him, "but I've had just about enough of Francesco."

That conversation is my fiction, but it's resting on fact. Before he knew what hit him, Frank found himself sailing across the Atlantic on his way to Bedonia and Compiano, the neighboring villages in Parma that were home to both the Serpaglis and the Marianis. I like to think that when he got there, his uncles taught him some respect.

Growing up in Charleroi, Gene would have seen all the latest dance acts. The Coyle Theater was part of the Keith Circuit—everyone in vaudeville played there—and if vaudeville wasn't enough, there were also the touring medicine shows that brought their own brand of hilarity to town. Throughout his childhood Gene was sopping up the good old American hokum he would teach his students and reproduce in amateur theatrical events for the rest of his life.

He would have seen buck dancing, the Black Bottom, the Cake Walk, and the Shim Sham Shimmy. He would have seen kids on the stage not any older than he was—so many kids that the Society for the Prevention of Cruelty to Children was getting to be deeply concerned—and he would have seen seasoned performers who did stunts that didn't seem humanly possible. He would have liked soft shoe, but the clog would have knocked him out.

In the sixty or so years since that princely black man Master Juba had emerged from the crazy, violent Five Corners neighborhood of New York to dazzle folks with the style of dancing they called "Pattin' Juba," rhythmic dancing had evolved into a breathtaking display of pyrotechnics. As Ireland met Africa, clog dancers were already using many of the steps my daughter would learn— the time steps, buffalos, maxifords, and wings—but it wasn't codified yet. They were still making it up as they went, looking for any new trick that would blow the audience out the back door. We're not talking *art* here, friends and neighbors, we're talking *entertainment*. You leapt onto the stage and you knocked 'em dead.

They ringed the stage with eggs and danced between them. They danced with canes, chairs, and shovels. They danced fight routines with each other, taking fabulous pratfalls. Doing what they called "acrobatic clog," they soared into the air, did flips, somersaults, and splits. Sometime around 1910, some forgotten hoofer thought of nailing bits of metal onto the heels and toes of his shoes to get a louder, harder, sharper sound. And on one of those nights in Charleroi, Pennsylvania, there must have been some particular burst of rhythm, some particular display of high-flying mad agility that left my father wordless with delight, his mouth hanging open in a big fat zero. "Say," he must have thought, "I'm going to be a dancer."

The center of everything in Charleroi was the McBeth-Evan glass plant where Gene's father and brothers worked. Eugene F. had brought Eddie and Louis down from Montréal to learn the ancient, respected, and highly skilled craft of glassblowing. There would have been no doubt in Gene's mind that, when he was old enough, he was going to learn it too.

Glass! That peculiar substance took me onto a fascinating side trip—swept me back into the stuff of a fantastic medieval romance—when glassblowing was a subbranch of alchemy, when every furnace, the "Glory Hole," had a magical salamander living at the bottom of it, when glassblowers guarded the secrets of their arcane craft and passed them on from father to son.

If you were a glassblower, your first loyalty was to other glassblowers—even though they lived in a different kingdom or principality, even if they professed a different faith than yours. Glassblowers formed powerful guilds, married into each other's families. Kings and dukes granted privileges to glassblowers they would grant to no one else. Glass was as valuable as silver or gold. Glass—shiny and smooth as a polished gemstone, hard as granite and fragile as an egg shell, transparent or translucent, blown into simple elegant curves or fabulously twirled, clear as ice or passionately colored—things made of glass must have looked to the people in the middle ages like objects retrieved from dreams.

When my father was a child, glassblowers were still something of an aristocracy among American industrial workers. European glassblowers were in such demand that many companies paid them top dollar and even allowed them to bring their trade union organizations to America. Proud men, glassblowers sometimes wore their dress clothes to walk to the plant; once there, they would hang their suits up neatly, work their shifts, and then put them back on again when they walked home. They were good solid family men; loved social clubs, music, and dancing; played in their town's bands and encouraged their children to play too.

Many glassblowers brought their socialist or syndicalist ideals with them. Eugene Debs, the Socialist candidate for president during the second half of the nineteenth century, always got lots of votes in the areas around glass plants. The socialist French-language newspaper, *L'Union Des Travilleurs*, had been published in Charleroi since the turn of the century. The French Socialist Federation of the Socialist Party of America—organized to connect French, Belgian, and French-Canadian workers—would be organized in Charleroi in 1912. Traditionally frugal, French-speaking glassblowers sometimes saved their pennies, banded together, bought their own plants, and ran them as socialist collectives. Even if Gene's papa wasn't a syndicalist or socialist, he was certainly a good trade unionist.

Glass plants were hot, dirty, and dangerous—and working in them was not good for you. Glassblowers who were afflicted with silicosis and related lung problems died young. Boys were routinely employed in glassmaking. The muckraking journalists of the Progressive Era, eager to reform the child labor laws, paint such a lurid picture in such highfalutin rhetoric that it's hard to get at the truth behind their descriptions of pathetic little boys as young as nine, the blood seething in their brains from the hellish heat of the furnaces, dropping into the snow outside the plant, too exhausted from hours of repetitive labor to walk home. Some of the photographs attached to these stories undercut the written arguments—the boys in them are skinny and grimy, it's true, but they don't have the air of exploited wage slaves. They're grinning madly at the camera. They look self-assured and cheeky as all hell. They're learning the craft from their fathers—just like Louis and Eddie.

Always chasing the top dollar, glassblowers were ready to move at a moment's notice. Sometime after 1910, Eugene F. received a better offer and moved himself and his family to Follansbee, West Virginia, to work for Jefferson Glass. He died there at forty-two, probably of silicosis. I'm looking at him in the somber photograph taken in Montréal just four years earlier, trying to read his sad dignified face—a good working man. With his small pipe cocked in his mouth and a straw boater on his head, Eugene F. might have looked jaunty in happier times.

I know the little houses fronting on the Ohio River—the ones that would have been cheap enough for working people to rent. I spent the first eight years of my life in one of them, visited relatives in others—houses so old that they still had the brackets for gas lamps screwed to their walls. Those houses had back bedrooms, so that's where I'll put Eugene F.—the dying man.

Gene is twelve. Bleeding my own childhood into his, I visualize the sick room with a rag folded over the shade on the lamp on the bed table to make a smeared light as yellow as old butter. I see godawful wallpaper, faded and stained with age, maybe roses, huge twists of ugly purple. The room stinks of camphor from the boiling kettle. Rags are folded neatly on the dresser—the rags that Papa coughs into. Afterward they'll be boiled with bleach. We're back in a time when doctors speak of *the crisis*—to live, you have to turn a crisis. The standard line is "If he can last through the night . . ." If Gene is like me, there are times when he can't stand to be in that house for even a minute longer. I see him walking for hours on the River Road.

Dying of silicosis, Eugene F. would have coughed for months before he lay down and couldn't get up again. Eugene F.'s mother, Marie Louise, came down from Montréal to help out, and she sits with him. Someone is always sitting with him—his wife or his mother or his stepdaughter, Olga. Approaching the back bedroom, Gene hears the dry rattle of breath, the steady rasp of it, and then the wracking cough that solves nothing. Sometimes Papa does try to get up. They have to hold him. He doesn't know them, his eyes hurt. He can't say anything. He's drowning. Gene can't hold his father's fear; it's deeper than anything you can pray about.

People come and go. Women whisper in halls. It goes on so long that it's a blessing when it's over, that's what everyone says. If Gene is like me, he thinks, no, it's not a blessing.

Houses are quiet after death. Someone makes coffee. Old Doc What's-his-name comes by and fills out the paper. Eugene F.'s wife and his mother take Olga with them into that back bedroom. Working together, they fold down the bedclothes. The dead man is revealed then, all of him, in his nightshirt. They will make him ready for the undertaker so he can be laid out in the parlor for people to see, to pay their last respects. In the few photographs we have of him, we can see him growing thinner as he approaches his death. Without speaking, his wife, his mother, and his stepdaughter wash him, wiping away the sweat and the dirt of his sorrow. They close his eyes.

Gene, years later, would hide his feelings behind a short

declarative sentence—"My father died young." Olga, years later, would tell the census taker that her father was born in France— forgetting Ludovico Serpagli and honoring Eugene F., the only real father she had ever known. This dead man is my grandfather. On a bitterly cold autumn afternoon, Mary photographed me and J.R. standing by the bare plot of ground where he's buried in the Brooke County Cemetery. Eugene François Maillard—born in Lyon, France, 1871, died in Follansbee, West Virginia, September 20, 1913. His family couldn't afford to mark his grave.

No, Gene's teenage memorabilia had not been thrown away by accident. He'd erased that part of his life—I was sure of it now. He was clever about it. He deliberately left no trace, not a clue. But I'd finally pinned him down. He was not a song and dance man from Pennsylvania. He spent his teenage years—lonely and without a father—trying to make sense of everything, staring at the lights reflected in the Ohio River. He was a poor boy from West Virginia just like me.

The doctor left his bill. The rent has to be paid. The house is cold, and they need a load of coal. There's nothing to eat but cabbage and potatoes. And there's no money. Gene knows that he's got to learn to do something, but it's not going to be glass. Gene hates glass. Glass sucked Papa's breath.

17.

"EDDIE WAS A VERY GOOD MUSICIAN." That's the first thing that Eddie Maillard's eldest daughter, June, tells me on the phone. It's spring, 2009, and she's talking to me from her home in southeastern British Columbia. "He had a whole lot of saxophones, but he liked the alto sax best."

After his father's death, Eddie just stuck around in Follansbee for the moment and continued to work for Jefferson Glass. Then, always on the lookout for the top dollar, he moved on to blow glass in Point Marion, Pennsylvania. Meanwhile, back in Canada, the Dominion Glass Company of Montréal had built a new plant in Redcliff, Alberta, and sent out a call for skilled blowers. Eddie, along with a half-dozen other glassworkers from the Ohio Valley, answered the call.

By 1916, Eddie was in Alberta where he met and married a local girl—Aggie Oakland—and fathered three daughters—June in 1917, Eugenie (called "Sis") in 1919, and Laura Mae in 1926. Louis, after being discharged from the US Army in 1919, joined his brother at Redcliff Dominion. The band June is describing is the one she remembers as a child.

> It was run by Daddy. He was the head boss. There were five or
> six musicians who played, all male, but a girl piano player. They

practiced at each other's house, brought the music. In the summer they played for outdoor dances—in the Hat, in the pavilion. It was covered at the top, and it had a good floor for dancing. They played there every Saturday night. They had to quit at midnight, because there was no music on Sunday. They had a piano—a box on wheels—and they'd lock it up every night. It was on one of the main stages. One time I coaxed Daddy to let me go with him. He had a big rug and three or four blankets, and I sat on the rug and wrapped up in the blankets, and I listened to the music. We only stayed 'til twelve.

Getting ready for a practice, they put their music on the chairs. It was in the living room, and one time they had to go uptown, and I took all the songs and wrapped them up in a big bundle and put them down the toilet . . . the outdoor toilet. So they had no music that night! Oh, he scolded me. He never slapped me, never believed in paddling the bottom. You got a punishment, stayed in, were not allowed to go outside or into the yard for a week. Couldn't play games or anything . . . Daddy always played music when he wasn't working.

I hear her hesitate. "Do you really want to know about Eddie?" I assure her that I do. "Tell me again who you are."

"I'm Keith Maillard, your first cousin. Gene Maillard was my father . . . Eddie's half-brother. I'm writing about my father's life. I think that Eddie would have been very important in my father's life."

"Oh. Well, what do you want to know?"

"Anything you want to tell me."

"Well, Daddy was good at his work—glassblowing. He made chimneys. He'd go in on the weekends and fool around. He made things for fun—you know, like ashtrays. I remember him the most of any of us. He spent a lot of time with me. He was a good guy with me."

Now her words are flowing quickly and easily. She's talking about her little sister. "She was very sick. There were two times when everyone thought she'd be dead by morning. My mother couldn't spend any time with me, so Daddy took care of me. He worked at the factory . . . four hours on and four hours off. The man next door, Charlie, arranged for the four hours off. Between those two men, they took care of me. I was around four. I stayed with Dad quite awhile . . . Sis needed all the attention. Dad would take me over to the factory, sit me on the window ledge. Guys were gathering glass . . . Do you know anything about how they blew glass?"

"Yeah, I do . . . a little bit."

"The gatherers would come over and have me take a puff on the pipe . . . 'Just a little puff, June. That's all right.'"

That would have been the chimney shop. I've read descriptions of how highly skilled glasswork was done. The gatherer used a pipe about three feet long with a bulb on the end of it, thrust the bulb into the Glory Hole—a two feet square cut into the brickwork above the furnace block. The heat there would have been fierce beyond belief. Then the gatherer wound the molten glass around the bulb until he had the right-sized ball. They were paying him good wages to be able to feel the right size. In one of the interviews I read, an old timer said that gathering the glass onto the pipe was "like trying to hold molasses on a broom handle." The gatherer then carried the pipe into the shop and took the first blow. That's when he would have offered the pipe to the four-year-old girl sitting on the window ledge. June would take a little puff, and then he would hand the pipe to Eddie, the blower, her father.

Eddie didn't blow into a mold. He would have done all the shaping by hand, all the work free-form—enlarging the glass, rolling it, stretching it—putting the individual touch of an individual man on every piece he made. He would have used the same tools that glassblowers had been using for hundreds of years.

He refired the bottom to smooth it out, blew into it again, used tongs to draw the chimney to its proper length, to get the size of the base exactly right, measuring it with a gauge. Then he set it aside to cool. Finally he tapped it on the table to snap it cleanly off the rod. That was the tricky part of the process because the cooled glass could shatter easily, and he would only get paid for a good chimney. The finishing boy collected the chimneys, heated them yet again, and crimped the sharp edges where the glass had been broken off.

In all of the accounts I've read of them, glassworkers were high-spirited, fun-loving men. They swapped yarns, yelled at each other, argued about the same things working men have always argued about—religion, politics, and sports. They sometimes broke into song. They kept buckets of water in the chimney shop, and when the heat in the shop got to be too much, dumped them on each other's heads. The guys in the chimney shop at Redcliff Dominion taught little June to cuss.

"They'd say, 'How many swear words can you say today?' They taught me to string out those cusswords, and I'd get a quarter and put it in my bank. It was all innocent enough—not that they'd care."

But June's mother cared. Aggie put June in the little red wagon and dragged her over to the plant, told the men in no uncertain terms not to teach June any more swear words. "We don't want any of your money."

But June yelled, "*I do!*" In telling me the story, she's found her child's voice—sings out the words exactly as she must have as a bright four-year-old—and I laugh. The men promised Aggie that they wouldn't teach June any more swear words. Instead they gave her money for singing little songs, or reciting poems—things like "Little Jack Horner"—and so June sat there on the windowsill and watched the whole process.

I'm not sure if June remembers who I am. Now the story itself is carrying her along.

Mother was a quiet person. Daddy was an extrovert . . . always smiling. He had one tooth taken out where you could see it. He was fun-loving. He'd take me driving in the car when we didn't have anything to do. I'd sit on his lap and steer, pretend I was driving the car. One day, he hit a bunch of ice. There were kids on the other side of the road . . . going to walk in front of us. I could see them, but I didn't know how to stop them, so I blew the horn. I just blew it like crazy. Daddy was busy with the wheel, and he said I'd done exactly the right thing. It made me feel good.

He wouldn't take me fishing on his boat. "No," he'd say, "it's too dangerous for a kid." Then eventually he said, "Okay, you can come out today. Get your rod, your equipment ready, you can fish." We went out, and I got restless. There was a nibble on the line. I caught a nice-sized fish. I had to take it off the hook myself. I caught one and nobody else did. I was proud of that.

Dad bought a house at Water Lake, kind of a ritzy campground. We went out there a lot of times. Dad would take us out there, go in and work again, and come back out. We had a U-shaped shed on the side of the house, filled it with straw and ice. We'd take fish and frogs and keep them there. I loved fishing, and I also loved catching bullfrogs for eating. They're very tender. They taste like chicken. We'd clean them up, take the hind legs off, not skin them. You skinned them before you cooked them. You just eat the back legs of frogs. Dad would give away frogs to friends.

There were two months in the summer when the frogs were lively. It was at night time when we'd catch them. There was a slough in front of the house—millions of frogs. I did things that ought to be done by a boy. I acted like a boy. I'd walk out with

my feet in the swamp, with my pail, and get the bullfrogs. The
bullfrogs were the only ones that croak. I'd smack one and put
it in the pail. I liked that fine.

She pauses a moment, then says, "He was a wonderful father to
me." For a moment I'm so choked up I can't speak. I hadn't known
that I'd been searching for a good father until I'd found one.

While I was interviewing Eddie's daughters, I dreamed that I was
a little boy. A man came into my room and stood at the foot of my
bed. I sat up and looked at him. He'd been standing there quietly,
watching me while I slept. He said, "I am your father." I knew that
he had to be Gene, but he looked like Eddie. I got out of bed, and
we hugged each other. When I woke up, I realized that I had never
in my entire childhood hugged a man. That's all I ever wanted, I
thought, that acknowledgment.

18.

GENE GRADUATED FROM HIGH SCHOOL in 1919. "I taught myself tap routines," he tells us about his adolescence—and nothing else. If he ever experienced the hard, hot, dirty, dangerous industrial work he would brag about later, that's when he would have done it—during those grim six years after Papa died. I still can't see him in a steel mill. I'm guessing that he worked at Jefferson Glass, part-time and summers, and hated every minute of it.

His sister and mother must have sweated blood to keep him in school. Olga never got beyond the eighth grade. She'd gone to work at fourteen and had been working ever since—cleaning other people's houses. Clementine might have found herself work outside the home too, but I don't know. The only thing that's certain is that every penny would have counted. Gene must have been ecstatic when he was accepted into Bethany College. That's when his small family split three ways.

Olga got married that year—to a local boy, Glen Wade—and would live in the Follansbee-Wellsburg area for the rest of her life. Clementine moved to Pittsburgh to help out her nephew, Joe Bertoli. He'd lost his young wife to the Spanish flu, which left him with two little girls who needed mothering and a boarding house to run. Gene hopped aboard the little local train—the "Toonerville Trolley," the students had nicknamed it—and rode it forty-five minutes through two tunnels and the wild West Virginia countryside to make his new home on the picturesque campus of Bethany College.

My father was expelled for putting a cow up a bell tower. A tall tale, right? That's what I'd always thought, but no. Campbell Tower has no bell in it, but there had already been a cow up there—in 1891—and the crazy freshmen who'd done it had long been honored in Bethany legend. They'd left a sign on the cow—"Beef is UP!" Of course my father would have joined a fraternity; he would have been drawn instantly to the daft rituals and systematized, sophomoric fun. Attempting to re-create the stunt with the cow would have seemed a perfectly delicious fraternity prank.

There was no shortage of cows—the Bethany College Farm had a whole herd of Guernseys. As anyone who knows the ways of cows will tell you, getting a cow up the one hundred and sixty wooden steps of the Campbell Tower would not have been terribly difficult. You'd need a couple of fellows in front to pull on the rope and a couple more in the back to give Bessie a good swat from time to time, or, if necessary, to twist her tail. Getting a cow back *down* one hundred and sixty wooden steps, however, is an entirely different matter.

The boys in Gene's fraternity had sworn to stick together through thick and thin—one for all, and all for one—but when Gene stepped forward like a man to own up to the fabulous deed, his brothers were nowhere to be seen. We should not pass over this moment lightly; we're talking about the waste of two and a half years and his family's hard-earned savings. When I visited Bethany in 2000, I found that my father's student record had been purged of everything but his name—misspelled. He was bitter about it for the rest of his life.

After his disaster at Bethany, Gene dusted himself off and got on with his life. The 1922 Charleston, West Virginia, city directory lists him as the manager of a restaurant called Maillard's. Nothing I have learned about Gene links him to the state's capitol, so I have no idea why he was there, but given the times, I'm guessing that his restaurant might actually have been a speakeasy. At any rate, the restaurant business must not have agreed with him. After its long silence, the black scrapbook becomes chatty again—"Maillard paid for two years of studies at Carnegie Institute of Technology in Pittsburgh by teaching tap dancing as an elective course."

A tap dancer is a percussionist. In December of 1922, Gene played the timpani at a concert given by the department of music at Carnegie Tech—probably his closest encounter with "legit" music. He was studying drafting at Tech and taking music classes there too—doing so well that he was allowed to sit in the last chair of the percussion section as the Tech orchestra churned out bits of Mozart, Grieg, Wagner, and Bach.

Gene's own band would have been closer to his heart. The College Wanderers was a seven-piece outfit—piano, violin, trombone, two saxophones, tenor banjo, and Gene on drums. In the photograph he pasted into the black scrapbook, he's sitting behind the rudimentary drum kit that we can see in almost any picture of early jazz bands, wearing a small self-satisfied grin that says, "Hey, boys, ain't this great?"

The oboe resting on the floor near the feet of one of the reeds players would have been used for slow syrupy love tunes, but more often they would have been playing maniacally cheerful two-beat dance music with ragtime syncopations that would sound corny, ancient, and stiff to us. In their own time, the boys would have come across as delightfully young and as thoroughly modern as the flappers and sheiks in a Held cartoon.

Sometime in 1924—there's no date on it beyond Gene's handwritten entry—Gene's engagement to Miss Lynnette Rose Cochrane, "a popular member of the Dormont younger set," was announced in a Pittsburgh paper. The Cochranes had just moved to Cleveland, but Gene didn't follow immediately. On New Year's Eve, he attended a dinner dance given by the South Hills Chapter of the Sotis Orir—the wacky name indicating a light-hearted social club, probably a fraternity of students from Carnegie Tech.

The logo of Sotis Orir was a skull inside a diamond; genial Gene was their president. The fraternity was graced on that sparkling New Year's night by the appearance of Miss La Vern McCrea, "an exceptional toe dancer of unusual ability," who danced a solo and then was accompanied by Gene himself in "a Flirtation Tango and an Apache Dance." Inside the program is an advertisement for the Barth School of Dancing—"Dancing taught in all its branches. Ask Gene Maillard." It was the same school where that other dancing Gene in Pittsburgh—Gene Kelly—had studied only a year or two before.

I'd always wanted to find Lynette Rose Cochrane, my father's first wife. "Why?" Mary said, "she's not even related to you. You're just obsessed with her because she's a pretty girl."

Well, that was true enough. I'd been fascinated by sweet-faced Lynette with the gardenia in her hair since I'd first seen her picture, but finding Lynette seemed an impossibility. She'd apparently never been listed in any US census.

Mary does much of her work at night. When the insomnia demon is riding her, she turns into an internet wanderer, refuses to let go, tries by sheer force of will to get the computer screen to yield up its secrets. Some of her best moves are mistakes. It was after two in the morning when she typed "Lynette Rose" and clicked on it before she'd added the last name. The search engine gave her a single result—Lynette Rose, born in Oklahoma in 1908, living in Dormont in 1920. W. G. Cochrane was her *stepfather*.

Mary tracked Lynette through her mother and Lynette's second husband. A few days later, I was having another one of those stunning phone conversations that didn't seem possible—I was talking to the daughter of Gene's first wife.

Lynette was an only child. Yes, she'd been a beautiful girl—she'd been a model for General Motors—and she'd always been mature for her age. When they put her in a convent school, she took all of her clothes off and ran naked through the halls, creating quite a scandal. Apparently the nuns had never seen a naked person before.

Lynette began dating Gene when she was fifteen and still at Dormont High. She hadn't been happy in high school. Lynette's mother had been understanding about her teenage daughter's romance with a man in his twenties. She'd thought that Lynette and Gene were compatible, and she'd been through much the same thing herself. Lynette dropped out of school and married Gene in the spring of 1925 when she was sixteen. They took off in his roadster, drove to Florida during the great land boom. "Mom was always ready to go places and do things."

Lynette told her daughters stories of that trip—no roads or bad roads, breaking down in the hills of North Carolina. Lynette was so afraid of mountain lions that she threw bits of her sandwich into the woods to keep them away while Gene laughed at her. That, of course, was during Prohibition, and Gene had stashed gin in the toolbox on the running board. They were stopped by a police officer. Lynette could scarcely contain herself as the cop stood there, chatting with them, taking his sweet old time, his foot resting on the toolbox.

Florida was the cat's pajamas. You could invest a thousand bucks in real estate and a year or so later sell it for *twenty* thousand—that was the popular wisdom—and maybe Gene had just such a get-rich-quick scheme on his mind, but he and his child bride arrived a year too late. Big slices of prime land were proving to be the watery dens of alligators; land prices were dropping off the map, and the "binder-boys"—those smooth-ass, fast-talking operators—were packing their suitcases and skulking away. Gene and Lynnette never set foot in any of the fancy hotels the developers had been slapping up, were instead the kind of tourists that Floridians hated and called "tin-canners"—the ones who ate beans out of cans and camped by the side of the road. I see them lying on the beach, drinking bootleg gin. Luckily they were back in Cleveland when a murderous hurricane raged across Florida in 1926 and delivered the final death blow to the great Florida land boom.

No, they'd never had any children. There was a story that Lynette might have lost twins, but no one knew if there was any truth to that or not. Lynette told her daughters that Gene had deserted her.

Mary called the courthouse in Cleveland to see if they had a record of Gene and Lynnette's divorce. Indeed they did, but the clerk wanted a formal, written request and legal proof of relationship. Mary had made her phone call on Christmas Eve afternoon, just before close of business. "Look," she said, "all I want is the date." The clerk relented—perhaps in the Christmas spirit—looked up the record, came back to the phone, and told Mary that Lynette had been the one who'd sued for the divorce. It had been granted on the 10th of October 1927.

The clerk now seemed just as fascinated by these dead people as we were. "Do you want to know what he did?"

"Sure," Mary said.

"Gross neglect of duty, nonsupport, and other acts of misconduct." Indignant, the clerk added, "She didn't even know where he was. They had to send the papers to his last known whereabouts." That was 177 Warrington Avenue, Pittsburgh—his mother's address.

Lynette filed for divorce at just about the same time that Gene was filing for a patent on his Theatrical-Make-Up Cabinet. Gene's meticulous drawing in Patent Number 1651898 is a fine display of the drafting talent that would guarantee him employment for the better part of his working life. The "Petite Amie" resembles an old-fashioned picnic hamper. With its neatly organized storage spaces, leather holding straps, built-in light bulbs, and pull-out mirror, it's a clever and useful invention. As Gene explains in his application, not only is the cabinet easy to use, but it can be closed up quickly, an important feature "in cases where a performance is concluded only a little while before train time."

Gene concluded his performance as a married man sometime in 1927. I could write the ending of their story several different ways, but Lynette would always be at the center of it, and she remains an enigmatic figure for me. That was the year when Elinor Glyn, the popular author of steamy romances, coined the term "IT girl" and hung it on the silent movie star Clara Bow. "IT" was that indefinable quality beyond mere beauty or sexiness that lit up a few choice girls with an eerie, irresistible, magnetic glitter. Lynette wears her hair and makeup exactly like Clara Bow's, has a face much like hers, but, to my eyes, is by far the prettier of the two—she certainly had IT.

It's one thing to play around with an IT girl, quite another to wake up to discover that you're married to one. Lynette, who was "ready for anything," might simply have been more than Gene could handle. Or, if she'd had a miscarriage, she might have been transformed from flaming youth to depressing misery. Or she might have been a bit of both, scarily unpredictable—up one minute, down the next—like the doomed wife in Fitzgerald's *Tender Is the Night*. But when a couple breaks up, it takes two to tango. Maybe Gene had become so addicted to the magical shadow-box world of the theatre that he hated to come home at night to face the messy realities of married life. I don't have enough information to commit myself to any particular story, but however you slice it, one thing is certain—Gene deserted his seventeen-year-old wife to pursue a career on the stage.

While Gene was becoming involved with Lynette, Eddie Maillard returned to Follansbee from Redcliff, Alberta. Glassblowers stayed in close touch with each other—often through their union—so the guys always knew who was paying top dollar, and that's what Jefferson Glass must have been offering to get Eddie to change countries once again, to uproot himself and his young family and move them several thousand miles away. June, who was seven, remembers the train ride from Redcliff as long, long, *long*. To Eddie's wife, Aggie, West Virginia must have seemed as alien as anything she might have imagined in the most God-forsaken outback of the British Empire.

The girls went to school in West Virginia for two years while Eddie did exactly what he used to do back in Alberta—blew chimneys in the daytime and played in a band at night. But June and Sis got to see something they never would have seen if they had stayed in Canada.

The Ku Klux Klan made a fire up on the hill. They were against the Catholics. It was on Saturday night, and everybody wanted to go out and watch what was going on, and they burned a fiery cross. It was burning quite nicely. The KKK walked around in a circle, in complete silence. I don't understand why men would do that. The next day Daddy took us up that hill, and we saw all the remains, the ashes. Oh, that was a steep hill!

I love Eddie for taking the kids up there in the light of day to show them that the cross had burned up just like anything else made of wood—that those sinister white figures hadn't been powerful magicians or ghosts but plain ordinary mean-spirited bastards dressed up in sheets.

June told me that the girls were not fond of West Virginia. "Sis and I used to sit out on the front steps in Follansbee and sing 'O, Canada' in the loudest voices we could." Their mother would come outside and say, "You girls shouldn't be singing that here. This is the United States of America. People don't want to hear that here." When she'd go back inside, they'd sing "God Save the King."

The first thing Eddie had to do when he arrived back in the Ohio Valley was square things with his grandmother—Marie Louise Paillet. "She was a fighter," June told me. "Not a penny's worth of anything got done unless it went through her. When we came down there, she told Daddy it was going to be a short visit and then out you go. But he found work and said, 'Look, we have to stay somewhere.'"

"Grandmother," June called Marie Louise, but she was her *great*-grandmother—and very much the grand-matriarch.

You'd go into her room and you would have to speak French. She had a bell. If she wanted Nini or Emilie, she'd ring the bell. They were so busy they couldn't be bothered, so one of us kids would have to go. Sis didn't go in very much. She was afraid of grandmother. So I'd go in there. I figured out pretty soon that there were three things that she wanted—tobacco for her pipe, peppermint candy, or toilet paper—so I'd try to figure out which one it was. I'd smell for the tobacco. There was a bag on the table. And I'd guess what she wanted. Look for the tobacco in the can. She'd give me some money. And I'd go down the street. She was a very demanding person. Sometimes she would reward me with a nickel. I couldn't understand her French. She spoke too fast and in a light-pitched voice.

Without a word of English, Marie Louise had come to a new country, to West Virginia, to help care for Eugene F., her sick son. After he died, she bought a boarding house in Follansbee, summoned her daughter Eugenie Brunet—Tante Nini—from Montréal to help her run it. Later on, she summoned another daughter, Tante Emilie Chazotte, to help out too. Tante Louise Battie came down for regular visits. Long after Marie Louise lost the ability to do anything but lie in her bed and smoke her pipe, she held the family together with her little bell—another of the enormously powerful women on both sides of my family who were at the stable heart of everything. In March of 1926, she died at seventy-seven.

I'm imagining that Tante Nini would have sent Gene the telegram. I can feel his annoyance—if he was like me at twenty-five, his family was the last thing on his mind—but that old lady was his grandmother, and he would have known his appearance at her funeral was a command performance. "Don't worry, honey," I imagine him telling Lynette as he climbs into his roadster or boards the train. "I'll only be gone for a day or two." No, he would not have considered taking Lynette with him.

That would have been the first time all of the living Maillards would have been gathered together in one place since old Louis died in Montréal. June and Sis were not allowed to attend the funeral, but they remember their grandmaman laid out in the living room so that the family and friends could pay their last respects. Money was too tight to ship Marie Louise Therese Paillet Maillard back to Montréal to be buried with her husband. She was buried with her son in West Virginia.

Gene Maillard and Eddie Maillard hadn't laid eyes on each other in ages and must have had a lot of catching up to do. Sometime during those stressful few days, they surely ducked out for a quick one. Eddie would have known the best local speakeasy—maybe one that sold genuine Canadian rye that wasn't watered too much—and the big man at the door would have known Eddie, opened to the code of his shave-and-a-haircut knock. Gene was too tight with his money to ever become seriously involved with alcohol, but he didn't mind a drop or two on occasion. Eddie would have needed a drink.

Now that I've put the half-brothers together, I have to imagine what they might have said to each other. These two very different men are often remembered with the same word—charming—so I see them faced-off and grinning, each doing his best to charm the other. Gene is talking to the big brother he'd idealized; he wants to impress the hell out of him. Eddie is harder for me to read. Maybe he's amazed at how Gene has changed, feels an uncomfortable mixture of envy and pride. Whatever is bothering them—and plenty is bothering them—my guess is that they're not talking about it.

We're at the height of 20s boosterism, a nutty time when Americans are chanting Émile Coué's self-help mantra "Every day, in every way, I'm getting better and better"—when ministers in mainstream churches are telling their congregations that Jesus was the first businessman and God meant us all to be rich—when it's commonly believed that any ambitious boy who sets his mind to it can make a million bucks. Not everybody believes that crap, but Gene does. Anybody who would drive a thousand miles to make it rich quick in the Florida land boom believes it. So of course he's telling Eddie about the theater—though he has yet to tread the boards.

Gene was never noted for his modesty. Now, at the height of his youthful arrogance, he's blowing his own horn with vigor and bravado. He's been working as a stage manager and set designer, he says. He's invented a clever machine to open and close the curtains, and it works like a charm. Maybe he sketches it out for Eddie on a scrap of paper. And he's been going to auditions too. Any day now he's going to start getting some good juicy roles. He's got talent. He knows the meaning of hard work. So it's just a matter of time. What could Eddie possibly say to that but "Good for you."

About himself, Eddie probably says, "I'm doing all right," but he's not doing all right. The days are long gone when he could float from town to town, blowing glass and blowing his sax, without a care in the world. Glass plants are getting to be automated just like Ford plants, and they've got machines that can do damn near everything now. They've even got machines that can blow glass just like a man, blow it into a mold. It used to take a lifetime to develop the skill to blow a chimney or a bottle or a window pane, but with these new machines they can train a man right off the street, and in a few months, he's doing the job just fine. Of course they're not going to pay him what they paid a skilled glassblower. Times are hard. Louis has given up on glass. Because he's a veteran, he's got priority for government jobs, so maybe he'll get something, but Eddie's stuck. All he knows is glass and music, and nobody makes a decent living out of music—not enough to support a family anyway. Eddie doesn't have to wait four years for the Great Depression. He's already in it. But Eddie doesn't want the conversation to get too serious, so he isn't talking about glass.

From everything I know of him, Eddie Maillard seems to have been a man who was all of a piece, but Gene Maillard, with his half a dozen hats, was a personality continually under construction. Eddie was the first musician in Gene's life—but I'll bet he was a lot more to Gene than that. How could we imagine any big brother more fabulous than Eddie? In every story I've heard about him I can feel his huge sunny personality. Not merely a musician, he was a man born with music in his cells. His golden saxophone was an extension of himself; he could make it talk. A natural athlete, he must have been the king of the sandlot; later he played semi-pro ball. I can see little Gene following him around, watching, learning to imitate the way Eddie talked, the way he walked, the way he teased the girls. Gene would have listened to Eddie's zany pick-up lines so he could try them out himself. As a grown man, Gene would resemble Eddie—at least on the surface. "Even if he wasn't smiling, he always had a twinkle in his eye" could have been said about Eddie as well as Gene—so could "He was well liked. He was lots of fun." But it feels to me as though charming Eddie was the original and Gene the copy.

I need daylight to end this scene, so I'll take the brothers out of the speakeasy and onto the street, headed back to the house on the river and the complex emotional tangle of family. We've all experienced those eerie balancing points when you can feel your whole life turning on a dime, and that's where Gene and Eddie are. Now that they've said all they can to each other—whatever it was—they're going their separate ways, into their separate silences. I know March in the Ohio Valley. For a moment or two the sun slides out from behind flat gray clouds, but it's watery, ineffectual, pale as an apple slice.

Gene already knows that he's in a bum marriage, but he hasn't yet figured out how to escape from it—hasn't yet realized that it's as simple as leaving one day for a rehearsal and then not coming back. If Eddie knows anything, he knows that the grand old craft of glassblowing is dying. He should stick with the job he's got at Jefferson, but Aggie is pregnant again, hates West Virginia and intends to go home to Redcliff to have her baby. So what's he supposed to do?

19.

Dear Aggie

I am up in Louis rooms writing this letter. I got my statement to day from the mill. You know they give you a statement about two days before pay day. I get paid thursday morning. I will send you every cent over my board thursday night. I dont know how much I am going to send you because I don't know how much Nini is going to charge me. Another thing I forgot to tell you is that you have to take out an insurance policy before they give you a job. They took 240 out of this pay. You got to pay one month in advance. If I should die you get one thousand dollars and I get 16 dollars a week for sick benefits so if I die you will be all right.

Say Aggie try and see Ed Walloff and see if he can get me a job laboring. Ill come right away. Im dying to see you and the kids. I cant stand this way of living very much longer. Well Aggie I guess this will suit you. I quit the saxophone for ever. I am trying to sell it so if I come back to Redcliff Ill be home with you all the time. Ill come right away if you can land me a laboring job.

Well Aggie by the time you get this letter I hope you have your baby. I dont care what it is boy or a girl. Well Aggie Ill quit. Ill write thursday night. Bye Bye sweetheart lots of love and kisses from

				Ed.

The next two letters are written on the stationery of the American Flint Glass Workers' Union of North America. There's no date on the first except "Friday Night."

Dear Aggie

I received the shirt to day and was glad to get it especially cause you made it yourself. It fits perfect. Aggie I sure wish I could get a laboring job at red cliff, Id come back right away. This is a hell of a way to live me over here and you and the kids over there. Its driving me nuts. I hardly ever move off the porch.

What makes me worse is I don't know how long it will be before I can see you again. If I should hapen to get word to come right away for a laboring job or any thing else, I could come right away because you know they keep two weeks back. I could leave on a pay day. That would be one hundred dollar. I wish my friend Ed Walloff could get me a job?

Well Aggie this is Sunday morning Ill try and finish this letter. Ive been so tired and disgusted I couldnd finish this letter. Ill try again.

Next Thursday is pay day, and every thing over my board Ill send you cause I know you need it. It might not be over fifteen dollars but it's the best I can do. You see it's a month since I started to work and I don't know how much my aunt will charge me for board but the next pay it will be quite a bit more. You know how it is. I need quite a few things myself

such as working shirts working pants and shoes but I can wait.
You can tell nurse Paterson and Mrs Gust that every thing will
be squared up about the time you get out of the hospital.

Aggie you don't know how hard it is for me to go to work
every day and not be able to see you, it aint right for me or you
to live like this. I would rather be out there with you even if I
had a hard job because it couldn't be harder than the job I got
here and nothing to live for. I am disgusted but Ill stick to the
job for your sake, because when you get out of the hospital I
don't want you to have anything to worry over cause you have
had enough already, and I think you are just fine for standing
up for all the hard-ships you already have had. It makes me
love you all the more to think what a good wife you have
proven your self to be. I wont forget it for a while. Since you've
been away Ive done the best I could but it wasn't very much,
and you never lost hope. Say Aggie let me know about how
much you are in debt counting groceries hospital and every
thing else. Ill try and borrow some money so you can square
up every thing so you wont be afraid to go out on the street
after you get better. Well I will close for this time kiss yourself
and the kids for me and try not to worry and take real good
care of your self.

Bye Bye Aggie lots of love and kisses for you and the kids
from Ed. (Hello June Hello Sis)

Thursday Night
Dear Aggie

I received your letter and was sure glad to hear from you. Louis
got a letter from Walter and says theres five chimney shops
working. Its funny Eddie Walloff didnt tell you to send for me,
tell Eddie. Ill take a job in the packing room if he cant give me

a place making chimneys because after the 15th if I dont come back Ill never be able to come back. Its then or never. |What will I do.| You better advise me and let me know right away. Well Aggie this is the first I missed work since Ive been sick. I had to come home this afternoon at 3 oclock. But I am going to work in the morning. You know this is on our last pay. Nini says the only thing the matter with me is that I need my wife to care of me. She dont know how you take care of me when Im sick does she or press my clothes. The way I feel now I dont care what comes or goes. I have tried to get back and I cant. So you will be the only one to suffer. But I dont want that to happen, thats why I want to go back. Louis wife is very sick. Personaly I dont think shell last long. (Keep that quiet.)

Things around here are going to be bad when the mill shuts down. I am stuck. I wont know what to do but if I cant get a job of some kind back there I guess Ill have to stay here. Listen Aggie please dont send me nothing for xmas Keep every thing you have. It costs too much for stamps and I always have to much trouble getting it. So dont forget.

How is my little June. I am sorry to hear youre not better of your sickness. What does Dr Patterson say about it. Why dont you ask him.

Well Ill close for this time. Dont forget to see E. Wallof. Try and get your self together so you can have enough milk for the baby. Bye Bye Love and Kisses to you all from Ed.

Hello June

Hello Sis.

Say Sis can the baby talk yet

Say June what grade is the baby at in school

The next letter, written in April 1927, is from Eddie's brother, Louis.

725 Main St
Sunday April 17

Dear Aggie and kids.

We got your telegram telling us what I wasnt expecting to hear.
We were pulling for him to get better, so that we could help you
financially when he got out of the hospital. We are in hard luck
now, but we felt sure that in a few months we would be out of
debt and able to help with some of your expenses. It hurts me
that I can't be there to see him. A little over 4 months ago, I saw
him get on the train in Steubenville. He was in apparent good
health then, and he was going to Redcliff to make a new start.
Sickness prevented him from a chance to make a start. I'm sure
he would have proved to be different than what he used to be,
had not sickness laid him low.

It is not my intention to make this letter gloomy. You
need to be cheered up, you have your life ahead of you, and
the future of your children depends on you. I know that you
have your hands full, it is not easy to earn enough money at
sewing to bring up a family of 3, but I know that you will show
the same willingness in the future that you did in the past, to
provide for the little ones. It is early to propose what I'm now
going to suggest, but Nell and I were talking it over, and if you
find it impossible to get along, on whatever sewing you can get,
if you want Nell and I to take either June or Sis, I want to assure
you that either one will not be mistreated. I know that you
won't care to part with any of your children, but you may not
see your way clear later on to carry on and feel strong enough
to work and provide for them. In that case, Nell and I would
gladly take one of the kids.

I preached to Ed about insurance and he could never see
it. I know that he left you without a dime, not even enough

for a decent burial. I know without going into figures that you have a hard road to travel, and that you are starting heavily in debt. I'm sorry that my debts forbid me to do the things I want to do. I know that in a few months, I should gain a lead on myself, then, when that time comes I will do whatever I can, be it ever so little, to help you out of your debts. Nell is never well, but I look for improvement in her condition from now on.

When you find time, I wish you would send me details of the funeral, pictures if you have any, of the grave. We are moving into a flat on Main Street next week, over the picture show, (opposite Cecelone's Store). We have no furniture of our own, but we are going to housekeeping with Nell's mother's furniture. Nell's mother is coming, to take care of her. We are too poor to afford a down payment on household goods on the credit plan, so, you see that we cannot do anything while we throw off the debts that have piled up on our shoulders.

I have worked steady since I began to carry mail last June, and I was obliged to borrow $75.00 at bank yesterday, after paying one for 150.00. If it is the truth about luck changing, then a big change is coming to us all around. You are deserving in better fortune than you have had in the past, and Nell joins me in wishing you everything that is coming to you. We hope that you will have the strength to hold up to put you in a position to afford a living for the kids, the ambition and willingness you always have had. Were I in a position to get away from my work and go to Redcliff and bring you back here, I would be on my way now. The distance from here to Redcliff is too far for one to be at the funeral in time. If any of your friends take pictures, I know you will remember me. If you could send me a picture of Ed, as he is laid out, perhaps in all your sorrow, you did not think of taking such a picture, or having someone take it.

Nell will write later, and she joins me now, in wishin you strength to carry on alone, for the time being, until we are able to assist in some way.

Louis

A few days after his first letter, Louis wrote again. The "Flints" he refers to are the guys in the glassblowers' union.

Follansbee WVa
April 22

Dear Aggie.

Just a few lines, it is late and we have been preparing to move. We're going to housekeeping to-morrow with Nell's mother's furniture, it is the only way that we can get away from light housekeeping. I note all you have to pay, and I knew you would stick with him to the end. I know what a shock it was to you to see him covered up in the hospital. The Flints I'm sure made things easier for you to bear, they are that way wherever there are Flints.

I wish you would send me something of Ed's as a keepsake, some little thing that you can ship in an envelope. I'm not asking anything valuable, but just any little thing, even if it is only a shirt button we value. Any clipping that you may find of the news of his death or of the funeral, I will appreciate very much.

Thanx for your sympathy extended to me for the loss of my only brother, and I want to assure you that you have mine, knowing only too well that you have nothing to carry on with but courage to face whatever hardships may come your way.

Ed had his faults, it is the usual thing to praise a man after he is gone, but his qualities outweighed his faults, and after all is said and done, Ed was a better man than he was given credit for being. He left here to make a new start, his illness and ultimate sad ending prevented him from showing the cockeyed world that he could deliver the goods once he made up his mind to do so. That was fate, and nothing else. He didn't have a fighting chance.

Must close, hope you will always enjoy good health, which added to your willingness, will help to insure a living for yourself and little ones.

Please remember my request for a keepsake, no matter how little it may be, value doesn't count. I will value anything that you will send that once belonged to Ed.

Nell joins me in extending best regards to you, father mother, sisters and kids.

Louis

The doctors in Redcliff said that Eddie died of Hodgkin's disease, but members of his family are still speculating about whether that was what killed him. He was thirty-three years old. I find it sad that Louis considered Eddie his "only brother," forgetting his little half-brother, Gene, but after all, Eddie and Louis were full brothers, bonded by the tragedy of their mother's death and their Montréal upbringing.

When Eddie died, Gene was in rehearsal at the Ohio Theatre for his role as Froggy in "Twelve Miles Out." Gene taped the Ohio Theater's May 22, 1927, program for "Merton of the Movies" into his black scrapbook and then nothing else until he and his "gum band" played in Pittsburgh in February of 1929. Except for the gaping hole of his high school years, that's the longest absence of memorabilia in the black scrapbook, and, once again, I'm stuck with trying to read something from nothing.

The year 1928 was the only year Gene didn't have a regular day job, so if he taught tap dancing in New York, as he said he did, that must have been the year when he did it. He might have sat in as a drummer with a few pick-up dance bands, turned up for every cattle call for every dancing gig or comedic role on Broadway or off, or plodded from office to office on Tin Pan Alley trying to flog his songs, but I don't know what he did. Insofar as the 20s actually roared, 1928 was the height of the roar—the shortest skirts, the craziest stock market speculations, the hottest jazz, the wildest parties. Musicians and entertainers have left us their memoirs, telling stories of driving madly from town to town, chasing shows and easy ladies, drinking their faces off, and I could write a story like that for Gene, but I'm not going to. I'm going to leave 1928 exactly the way Gene left it—a blank—except to say what I do know. Eventually he would have heard that his brother Eddie was dead.

20.

IN 1929 GENE WAS BACK IN PITTSBURGH, living with his mother. I can sympathize with him. I know what it feels like to ride your life out to such a nowhere that all you can do is to go slinking back to Mom. He was nearly thirty, and he'd accomplished not a damned thing. He must have felt worthless, an utter fraud.

It's hard to keep going when nobody believes in you, but Gene gave it another try. Early in the year he slapped together an ensemble of out-of-work musicians and put on a show billed as "sixty minutes of foolishness by Gene Maillard and his gum band"—very much a low-rent gig, a fundraiser for the Pittsburgh Athletic Association. He would have planned the performance as the first of many such nights of fun and frivolity, imagining his reputation as the zany king of comedy spreading throughout Pittsburgh, but that band never played again.

By spring he was teaching at the Olympic Studio of Dancing. Their fat, slick program documents a booming business—a dancing mill for little girls, starting them out so young they could barely toddle across the stage, teaching them every conceivable terpsichorean exercise from toe to tango, tap to acrobatic. Gene sweet-talked his way into heading up the Olympic Dramatic Department, "the only one of its kind in any dancing school in the city." The Crash, in October of '29, put an end to that gig. The

Depression was not a time for pampering your daughters. Gene didn't collect any dance school or theater memorabilia for the next three dark years.

The lovely showgirl, nineteen-year-old Ruth Jamerson, had been on the stage since she was three and wouldn't have needed dancing lessons, so she probably wasn't one of Gene's students. She might have been supplementing her incoming by teaching a class or two at the Olympic Studio, but we don't have to work hard to imagine her meeting Gene—they were both in show business and both living in the South Hills. From the timing of my brother's birth, I suspect that J.R. might have been conceived at a New Year's Eve party as the gloomy year, 1930, was drawing to a close.

Gene eventually got around to doing what he probably saw as the right and honorable thing—he married Ruth three months after J.R. was born. Then, six weeks later, early in 1932, his mother died.

Near the beginning of the black scrapbook Gene has pasted in two small, bleached-out photographs of his mother. In a group shot, Clementine is one of five women in baggy dresses confronting the camera from a patch of sunlight on a lawn. As my other grandmother often did, she's holding a tea towel scrunched up in one hand. Her white hair is pulled up into a bun, and she has the kind of old lady's wizened face you get when you carve a human visage onto an apple and leave it outside in the sun all day, so we guessed her to be in her seventies. When we received her death certificate, we discovered that she'd died at sixty-one. That photograph must have been taken in the last year of her life when she was already suffering from the disease that killed her.

The attending physician wrote out the cause of death in the hasty, maddening, illegible scrawl that doctors traditionally use on prescription pads, but Mary and I could make out enough of it to piece the story together. Clementine had breast cancer. She

would have been sick long enough—probably for months—for
it to have been a grinding daily misery, for both herself and for
Gene. She had a mastectomy, picked up a staph infection in the
hospital, and died of erysipelas of the breast—an excruciatingly
painful disease that can sometimes lead to gangrene. Antibiotics
would cure it today, but they hadn't even discovered sulfa drugs
yet. She would have suffered terribly.

Gene was at her side throughout her long dying. He signed her
death certificate. Her family reassembled itself in Pittsburgh for
her funeral—the Marianis and the Bertolis and all of her children.
Olga brought her ten-year-old son, Franklin Wade.

Gene had been married to Ruth for all of six weeks by then;
J.R. was not quite five months old. I remembered the very first
thing my cousin, Doctor Wade, had said to me when I'd called
him—"Of course I know who you are. I held you on my lap when
you were a baby." Later he'd talked himself out of the memory,
but I shouldn't have been so eager to help him. Yes, memory
can conflate or falsify events, convince us of things that never
happened, but it can also leave us with tiny brilliant images as
accurate as Kodak snapshots. The tall, kind, silent, "classy"
brunette my cousin remembered had been young Ruth with
unbleached hair. The baby he had held on his lap was J.R.

Gene had married Ruth with reluctance, yet he brought Ruth
and J.R. to Clementine's funeral. He was presenting them to
his family, making at least that much effort to take his marriage
seriously, but he must have been emotionally depleted, ground
down to the bone. Clementine surely had been the foundation
of his life. In the bitter month of February 1932, neither he nor
anybody else in the family had the money to pay for her gravestone.

Fifty years later, Gene would tell his Masonic brothers that after
his mother died, he disowned his family. He would point to that as
the moment when he'd first started to become a successful man. In

the darkest year of the Depression, 1933, Gene left Pittsburgh and moved in with his sister Olga and her family in Wellsburg, West Virginia. He had just disowned his wife and infant son.

The year after Clementine died, her son Frank Serpagli died too. His young common-law wife, Edythe Feigenbaum, signed his death certificate, listed her address as 177 Warrington Avenue—Clementine's house. Olga was Frank's full sister, so she almost certainly rode the train to Pittsburgh for his funeral, and possibly Gene went with her. The demonic boy who had tortured Gene had grown up to be an obnoxious drunk who worked as a projectionist—a boring blow-hard who bragged about the famous people he'd known in show business. Even his own sister would remember him as "not much good."

The physician who signed Frank Serpagli's death certificate had much better handwriting than the one who'd signed Clementine's, so there's no doubt about his opinion of what killed Frank—chronic toxic myocarditis. Frank died a boozer's death.

It takes a real effort—a pure and single-minded dedication—to drink yourself to death by the age of forty. Frank would have seen it coming. He would have awakened night after night, catapulted out of his drugged stupor by a ghastly sensation like a small animal trying to claw its way out of his ribcage. There would have been only one cure for terror like that—another drink, a quick one and a big one. Maybe he was the kind of drunk who paced the floor at night screaming at unseen tormentors. Maybe he took it out on his wife and kid. Maybe he had enough time at the end to yell "Jesus!" and clutch at his chest. Then he would have been felled as savagely and conclusively as if a stake had been driven through his heart.

He left behind a nine-year-old son and a girl he'd never married. Edythe was fourteen years younger than Frank. His son—another of the fatherless boys who keep appearing in this narrative—is listed in the 1930 census as Thedore. In 1942 he appears in Pittsburgh, in the Peabody High School yearbook with his name spelled correctly as Theodore, and we learn that his classmates called him Teddy. After that he vanishes from the public record.

Depression or no Depression, Gene managed to get himself a job—became a clerk in the cost department of Wheeling Steel's Steubenville plant. In June of 1933, Gene and his "Little Review" appeared at the Palace Theatre in Wellsburg. The program looks as though it was hand-crafted at the local grade school; the cover bears the motto: "Dancing is an art that cannot be mastered in a day." The *Daily Herald* in Wellsburg reviewed the show. "The juvenile artists of Gene Maillard's dancing school display talent in the benefit review. . . . Especially good was the tap work. Gene Maillard's showmanship was never more evident. He has put on some good shows but last night his material was even more pliant than usual."

Gene's "Little Review" played repeatedly in Wellsburg—and also in Brilliant, Power, and Follansbee. The programs list the kids' names, and I spent hours on the phone, trying to find any of them—and eventually succeeded. A lady in her eighties remembered my father vividly.

Gene taught tap in a bare room above the bank in Wellsburg, she told me. He charged fifty cents a lesson. It was the Depression, and nobody could afford tap shoes; you got an old pair of oxfords and had the shoe man nail taps to them. Gene was a wonderful teacher. He was patient and lots of fun, always had good jokes to tell. He made you believe you could do it. You always wanted to do your best for him. She and a boy from her class at school loved the lessons so much they'd walked around Wellsburg tapping everywhere they went. One afternoon they went to see her dad at work—she'll never forget this—and tapped all the way down the hall and into his office. Her dad really got a kick out of it. When

Gene stopped teaching in Wellsburg, she tried the next teacher who turned up, but she didn't stick with him because he wasn't any fun.

Gene met my mother in 1937. I'll bet he met her at a dance. She was a cute little blonde who loved to dance, and the dance floor was his natural environment. Lynette and Ruth had been too tall for him, but Aileen, at four-eleven would have been just right.

The key to surviving the Depression was having a job, and my mother had one. Gene would have liked and respected her for that. She worked with her brothers in the blueprint shop at Uncle Will's W. C. Brown Company. I used to hang out there when I was a kid, and I can easily imagine a scene—closing time on a chilly winter's evening, and Gene is meeting my mother to take her out to dinner. The moment he steps through the door off Chapline Street, he can smell the acrid chemicals used in the blueprint process. My mother can't leave yet because they're working on a rush order. By then Gene would have known that Aileen's brothers hated each other and never spoke, so he would have made friends with them separately. He and Addison were both Masons, and that would have given them an instant connection. Most people liked my uncle Bill, and Gene would have liked him too—would have shared a drink and a laugh with him at the Elks Club.

Tonight, as Gene steps into the back, he finds Bill actually working for a change. The blueprints come off the line in huge, continuous, wall-sized sheets of paper that need to be cut with long shears designed especially for the job. It takes two people. On one side of the table my mother starts by snipping the paper; then, once the cut gets going, she continues it by simply leaning across the table and pushing the shears forward. Bill, on the other side, does the same thing; if they've aimed right, their two cuts meet in the middle. With two skilled workers, cutting blueprints has its

own graceful rhythm, and Gene might have seen it as an odd kind
of dance.

Gene was picking up a few extra bucks wherever he could. He
was the breezy, fast-talking MC in a nightclub in the dirty little
steel town of Steubenville, introducing such acts as the "Summer
Frolic" and the "Jayne Jarrell Girl Show." A local boy named
Dino Crocetti could have been in the audience on any of those
nights—a rough young Italian-American boxer who would later
take up singing and call himself Dean Martin. Dino's pals and
associates and patrons would have been there too—the shady
characters floating up from the Ohio Valley's underside—and
Gene probably charmed them just the way he charmed everyone
else. My mother would have seen him as a man of the world, a guy
who'd been around the block and knew what was what.

If Gene was wise to the ways of nightclubs, he was just as
wise to the respectable daylight world. He had a good job at
Wheeling Steel. He was a Mason and a community entertainer.
He understood the values of those Ohio River towns; he'd grown
up there, and those were his values too. He gave the folks what
they wanted. The kids he taught in Wellsburg adored him, and
their parents liked him well enough to pay for dance lessons—as
he took his "Little Review" on a tour of school gymnasiums up and
down the river. My mother would have seen him as a man who fit
into *her* world—"well liked," she would have said.

"He's a good dancer," my mother surely told my grandmother,
which would have cut no ice whatsoever. "Does he have a job?"
was more to the point. Well, yes, he works at Wheeling Steel—and
in the evenings he teaches tap dance to children. I can hear my
grandmother's voice: "Well."

Mabel would have laughed at his jokes, and he must have
charmed her too; in a written note to me, she commended the
Maillards for their "gallantry." But, as my mother told me, "He was

so cheap he was still wearing the same suits he'd bought in high school." When my grandmother met him, those suits would have been twenty years old. Fashion-conscious Mabel Sharp, who could, in an instant, read people by their clothes, would have looked at those outdated, threadbare suits and thought, *shabby*. Depression or no Depression, there was no excuse for that.

When he tap-danced on the radio, my grandmother must have listened to his easy-going singing voice and the fantastic click of his heels. She would also have heard the announcer's affirmation that Gene was indeed employed at Wheeling Steel. "A regular mill man," he liked to call himself—a guy who was anything but.

He was *French*, was he? What would Mabel have made of that? There were no French people in the Ohio Valley—not that she knew of—so, by calling himself French, Gene would have placed himself outside any recognizable category. French meant what? Lafayette? Our gallant allies in the Great War? Maurice Chevalier? Like most other Americans, my grandmother would have seen that smooth and smiling song and dance man on the screen—wearing a boater and a tux, speaking English with a put-on French accent so thick you could paper the walls with it.

A Frenchman might be hard to place, but at least he wasn't a Wop or a Hunky, and my mother would have assured my grandmother that Gene wasn't a Catholic, but still . . . The Thomases had been here as far back as the first Reuben Thomas who'd floated down the inland waterways from Geneva in what he always referred to as "old York State." In the 1790s he'd cut "Reuben's Trace" out of the frontier wilderness of what later would become Clarington, Ohio. The Sharps had been here just as long; they'd been tradesmen and merchants in Ironton, another dot of an Ohio River town. No matter how you sliced it, my grandmother would have known that Gene *wasn't one of us*.

It might have been the first time in her life that my mother ever went against her mother's wishes. Aileen Sharp and Gene Maillard had both survived sorrow and despair. They'd lost eight of their prime years to the Depression. They'd worked hard, scrimped and saved, and played it safe. In 1938, she was twenty-seven and he was thirty-seven. It was a time for a change. It was a time for *them*. It was time to get married.

So they got married, and then what? And then nothing—and this is *The Big Nothing*. My mother deliberately destroyed all records of her marriage, and so, obviously, did Gene. In his scrapbooks he's presenting himself to the world as he wants the world to see him, so, after a nod to his French origins, the entertainer is very much front and center. With the single drawing of a breeder reactor at Hanford, he acknowledges his years as a draftsman. In case we might doubt that he's a genuine philanthropist, he fills up several pages with canceled checks. We know that he cares deeply about his students because he pastes in dozens of their pictures and then adds clippings about their successes later in life. He commemorates his first two wives for their cuteness—Lynette as a teenage IT girl and Ruth as a sexy showgirl—but his third wife does not exist at all. We can tell from the photographs that he likes children and they like him, but there is no record—not even the faintest hint— that Gene Maillard was ever a father.

Sometime during the four years that my parents were married, Gene stopped working at Wheeling Steel and joined the prestigious engineering firm of Sanderson & Porter, but I don't have an exact date for that. They had to live somewhere— probably in a little apartment in a low-rent part of town like East Wheeling—but wherever it was, I never heard about it. Was my mother still working? I don't know. She didn't leave me even the smallest fragment of an anecdote around which I could swing a story. What she would talk about was the Depression.

21.

I GRADUATED IN '29. That was the period that I turned against Dad. Everybody was going away to school in the fall, and I had my room paid for, reserved. We'd been saving money for years. Mother and I worked on clothes all summer. I had my wardrobe ready. I had these good-looking clothes to go to . . . I was going down to Athens, to Ohio University. I'd been accepted. I had my room. I'd corresponded with the girl I was going to room with. And Dad came home and says, "Well, you can't go. I lost all your money in a poker game." Says, "I was trying to get you double what I had . . . lost it all."

So that's that. I turned against him. I never forgave him, really. Even today, I can't . . . Because . . . Lord, Keith, I was college material.

I was crushed. It just knocked it out of me. Everybody . . . all the girls that I knew were going to college. Either up to West Liberty, or Bethany, or down to West Virginia. I didn't get to go. But . . . I was so crazy about P.A. In time it was just kind of a thing of the past. Mother never forgave him for building me up to the point of going to school and then coming home and saying, "You can't go." It was just one thing after the other like that, ah . . . and she never forgave him. That's really hard to do to a kid, you know. Especially an eighteen-year-old that had the world on a string. But . . . I survived it.

P.A. ended up dying in Kentucky. Well, you see . . . Aunt Olive. You know who she is? Well, she lived in Cincinnati, and she had money too, and P.A. got a job there. He was a shoe salesman. Good one. He knew shoes. He stayed with Olive, and he saved up his money and moved out and went to Covington, right across the river, which was a gambling center at that point. Everybody from Ohio—Cincinnati and all the little towns along there—went to Covington to gamble. They couldn't do it in Ohio, so they went to Kentucky.

Well, he stayed there a long time, and finally Martha went down. I think he called her, asked her if she would come down to see him. She told me later that she was appalled. He was old, he was thin, he was sick, and he didn't have anyone. So she took him home, and Harley says, "Well, he can stay until he's on his feet, but I'm not keeping him." So P.A. was in their home about six months, I guess, and he went back to Covington, and that's where he died. Martha kept in touch with him.

He worked in a gambling house, worked as a dealer. That's all he knew, was cards. If you'd played bridge, after the first bid around, he'd know what everybody had in their hand. Everybody. I was a good bridge player too. He taught me to play bridge. He knew cards. Whew! He always thought he could make his fame and fortune, but he was just a small-town gambler. Oh, boy. It was Martha that would call him, but you see, I couldn't have him write to me. Mother was so against the whole thing. She wanted no part of it at all. I never got a letter from him. He kept in touch with Martha. And still I was his favorite.

The Crash? Oh, that was rough. That was the year I graduated. Nobody spent a nickel because they didn't know where their next meal was coming from. FDR had what they called "a bank holiday." Everything was closed—banks, stores. It had something to do with the money—the dollar. How much the dollar was worth. That type of thing. You couldn't buy anything. Nobody had anything to sell. And it . . . it was a rough time. Everybody was trying to get their money out of the banks. Standing in line and screaming that they wanted their money and . . . If they got in, they demanded every cent. The public broke the banks. The banks don't keep all the money. They seem to have the idea you give the bank a hundred dollars, it better have that hundred, you know, back then. And it doesn't work like that and never did.

Well, we didn't notice it too much at home, I don't think. You didn't get dairy products like we used to, like cheese and butter and milk and that type thing. Something about the farmers, but don't ask me what, I don't know. But I do remember that the only way we got milk was because Mother knew these people up on Kirkwood Heights. Oh, Lord. We didn't have any extras. Money was tight. It was always tight when you get down to it, so it really didn't affect us that much. But there were things you couldn't get.

A lot of people out of work. Oh, yes. And food lines. There would be a hundred people standing in line to get a loaf of bread. The big companies like Hazel Atlas and Wheeling Steel—oh, they laid people off like crazy. They kept their offices open, but they got down to a skeleton staff. Everybody was hurting. Nobody was working right. Money was tight. You were lucky to have enough food, and, ah . . . churches, I guess, Salvation Army and all the . . . that type people . . . had soup kitchens. And people would stand in line. I remember St. Luke's down on the Island had the big one, and they would line up clear around the block to get a bowl of soup.

I wasn't allowed out alone, so what the street situation was, I don't know. But guys were showing up at the door, oh, every day. Two and three a day. Anything. A crust of bread. Mother used to make sandwiches and have them ready. And that gets passed along. You know, you give it to one person, and he goes out . . . "Go back to so and so." So you have a steady stream of people wanting a sandwich. Deserving people. They were really hungry, and they . . . That's when the soup kitchens started. Up until then, there was no great demand for handout.

We listened to FDR on the radio. Don't ask me what he said. I don't know. But you never missed his programs. Everybody sat around and listened to him, and you didn't dare talk while he was talking. It was like 6, 7 o'clock—early. It was after people that worked were home and before evening. Everything on the news was the Depression. People hurting. People wanting help. You know. I don't ever remember seeing world news at that point. Everything was local. World news there was, I'm sure, but everybody was concerned with their own little community and how they would survive it. Which they did.

So after Dad lost the money and I couldn't go to school, I went to work for Uncle Will Brown at eleven dollars a week. Uncle Will was the mainstay at that point, and he told Mother, he says, "You send her over." I was with Uncle Will as long as I could stand it.

Bill and Addison never could get along. Uncle Will of course owned the business, and he took Addison in, and Bill . . . Well, you see, when Bill graduated from high school, that was another disappointment for me—a big one. Bill was two years ahead of me, and so we moved down to Miami in Oxford, Ohio, so Bill could get a college education. Clara paid for Mother's moving. Addison drove us down, and we rented this house. It was a very nice little place. And Bill entered Miami, and I went to McGuffey High School. We were supposed to stay there while Bill went to college, and then I was supposed to go too . . . But Bill drank and played tennis. And dated and ran around. And he flunked out of there, so we moved back to Wheeling, and that was the end of that.

And then Bill went down to the Fostoria Glass and got a good job and drank himself out of it. So he came up, and he bellyached to Mother, and Mother to Aunt Deal. "Well, you just go in the shop and work with Addison." Which was definitely the wrong thing to do. I wasn't in there with them then. And, ah . . . I was out at the Hazel Atlas and should have stayed there. Skipper Cobb was my boss out there, and when I told him I was quitting to go out and take care of the shop and the books for Bill and Addison, he said, "Don't do it. Do *not* do it! I beg you, don't do it." But Mother was pushing, the Browns were pushing, so I went.

Addison and Bill worked together in that shop and never spoke a word to each other. Addison did photostats, and Bill ran the other part, the blueprint, and there was a man—can't think of his name—that came in about once a week from the Y and O Coal Company to have prints made, and he talked to me. I'd be at the desk, Addison would be at the back making photostats, and Bill'd be running blueprints, and he always had somebody else doing it because Bill didn't work if he could help it. And this man from the Y and O Coal Company, he got pretty damned smart. And I said, "If you don't back off and let me alone, I'm going to tell my brothers."

"Well, who in the hell are your brothers?"

I said, "Bill and Addison." There they were.

His mouth flew open. He said, "My God, you're not . . . They're not brothers!" He had been coming in there for years and didn't realize that they were brothers. And didn't know that I was a sister.

I said, "Yes, and they're *my* brothers." Because none of us were alike. When you stop to think of Bill and Addison, they were as different as night and day. And of course I was . . . nobody. But from that time on, that man was the nicest person I ever knew. He came in, he always waited . . . He was from out in Ohio, out beyond St. Clairsville, and he always took me to lunch. First time he asked me, I said, "Oh, I don't know."

He says, "Come on and go." He says, "I promise that everything will be okay . . . ," and he turned out to be a very nice person. I never told Addison or Bill. I couldn't talk to Addison at that point anyhow. Addison knew it all. And Bill didn't give a damn. He was drunk most of the time.

Bill was drinking like a fish, but he always had good clothes and dressed like a fashion plate. Bill wore clothes well. He was big enough to carry them. Addison, poor Addison, was raising a family, and he went to Richmond. They had $29.95 suits. Bill went to Bernhart's and paid two-*hundred* ninety-five for his.

Bill was flitting from bar to bar. You know what I mean? Bill would do anything—no, I won't say *anything*—if he didn't have to work. He made friends so . . . I don't know. Bill was a sponger. He was just like P.A. He expected somebody to take care of him. Which Mother did. All he wanted to do was just have the best clothes—which he had. And Mother would sit up till midnight sewing in order to keep food on the table, and he'd take ten dollars from her and go gamble. Bill was a . . . I don't . . . I won't use the word "favorite," but Bill could do no wrong in Mother's eyes. Drink. Gamble. "Oh, he's just like his father." You know, Bill was a likable person. And I liked him. I liked him ten times better than Addison. But he was a Sharp. He would not work.

My life wasn't what it should have been, because Dad was a gambler. He lost everything he made. Dad took everything from the Sharps, and Clara kept us. He didn't work. He just piddled around and gambled. That's the reason Mother left him. And Bill was very much the same type person. Mother was working, I was working, Addison was working, and Bill would not work. Bill would take bread of a person's mouth rather than earn it . . . and I resented it. I went through a period that I was bitter that I didn't have the backing that I should have had. But . . . it taught me a lot about men. It wasn't like today. Today's girls are on an equal footing with the men in business. They've earned it up through the years. But back then, ah . . . men expected a hell of a lot out of a girl. I'm surprised I made it.

After that affair with that man from the Y and O, I made it known to every man that came in there that Bill and Addison were my brothers. I thought, well, as long as they know that my brothers are here, they'll back off. Which they did. At that point in time . . . I don't know whether it's changed; I don't know anything about the business world today . . . but a man was out to get all he could get and didn't hesitate. I don't know how I ever got through all that. Well, I wasn't the only one. Every girl that worked at that point, and had contact with men, would tell you the same thing. A man would do anything to take advantage of a female, and a girl just had to fight her way through the years for respect. And it wasn't easy. And I couldn't go home and talk to Mother about it because she was at a place then that she wouldn't understand. So, my life hasn't been too easy. I've met a lot of very nice men. I've met a lot of scoundrels.

I shouldn't have spent seven years in a blueprint shop. I still have a pair of those big shears. About that long. I could do that too. I could start and go, and whoever was on the other side of the table could come right into it. I worked hard that seven years. That was a hell of a job. I was making twelve dollars a week. And Bill was taking every cent that came in. You'd go in on Monday morning, and he would have written a check for everything that was in the bank. Those were my hell years.

22.

ALTHOUGH THE NAME OF THE TOWN—Hot Springs, Arkansas—has been in my head for as long as words have been in there, it never occurred to me to think about the meaning of those words, to say to myself, "Oh, there must be *hot springs*"—as, indeed there are. The thermal waters flow from an ancient watershed at over 140 degrees Fahrenheit, but if my mother ever soaked herself in them, she never told me about it. By the time that she and Gene were living there in 1942, the town had been transformed from a popular spa for folks with arthritis into a rehabilitation center for sick and wounded servicemen—but she never told me about that either. The Hot Springs I heard about is the town as she remembered it—a miserable rural dump in the middle of the ignorant, stinking hot, crapped-out, nowhere South. She agreed to go there with Gene, she told me, "to save the marriage."

"There was no great love between us . . . either Gene for me or me for him. It was a matter of convenience at that point. I was pushing thirty and panicking. The fellas that I had run around with in Wheeling, I didn't want to marry. They were . . . stupid. I don't know. Gene had been around and in things. He was a different personality. We got along all right. But I couldn't live with his damned tight . . . His worshipping the dollar is what broke us up."

That is her summary, her official public statement delivered a lifetime later, but she also said, "Mother's the reason that your dad and I didn't get along," and even once, dropped as a sad aside while she was talking about something else, "I don't know what happened to us."

To say that they were trying "to save the marriage" implies that they'd talked about it, knew they were in trouble. I doubt that either she or Gene saw their marriage as "a matter of convenience"—at least not when they first went into it—but later, after it was over, she would hang that label on it to trivialize the experience, to push the pain away from her. The reason they split up is nothing that can be summarized in a few sentences. I grew up listening to her stories, and I don't believe that she ever really understood what happened in Hot Springs.

However much my father might have fancied himself an artist, a footloose entertainer, he liked his income to be reliable. Except for the last two years before the Crash—when he was playing stock comedic roles in Cleveland and then doing whatever he did in 1928—he always had a day gig. His first job of any consequence had been with the engineering firm of Sanderson & Porter in 1921. He worked elsewhere—most notably at Wheeling Steel—but Sanderson & Porter continued to employ him off and on for years. He must have proven himself just as reliable to them as they had always been to him; wherever they needed him, he packed his suitcase and went—to half a dozen towns in Pennsylvania; to Lake Charles, Louisiana; to Biloxi, Mississippi; to Hot Springs, Arkansas.

I can find no record of Sanderson & Porter doing anything in Hot Springs, but as soon as the war started, they landed a fat government contract to build and operate the Pine Bluff facility sixty-three miles away. Magnesium and thermite incendiary bombs were manufactured, assembled, and stored at Pine Bluff. Some of the bombs used to torch off Dresden might well have been manufactured there.

Pine Bluff didn't have just a weapons plant; it had an arsenal and an airbase. The minute the word had gone out that the big bucks were coming to town, folks from all over Arkansas had converged on Pine Bluff looking for work. They camped by the sides of the road, crammed into boarding houses, as many as fourteen men to a room. When the plant was fully operational, over six thousand people were employed there, and there was no housing to be had. The situation got so bad that the Army Corps of Engineers towed quarter-boats up the Arkansas River from Memphis and stuffed a thousand workers into them. My parents didn't live in Pine Bluff, but that doesn't necessarily mean that Gene wasn't working on the Pine Bluff project.

As a draftsman attached to the engineering department, Gene must have been one of the elite. The engineers might have set up offices in Hot Springs, close enough to Pine Bluff to send plans back and forth, or even commute when they had to, but well away from the overcrowded, frenzied activity of the weapons plant. They would have found adequate housing in Hot Springs, not just for single men but for whole families—and Gene had an entire house assigned to him. I imagine him walking to work to save money. I imagine him sitting in an office in his shirtsleeves. Maybe there's a Betty Grable calendar on the wall. I see Gene dipping the sharp nib of his pen in India ink and leaning into his drawing board. I've set this scene in the stifling heat of the Arkansas summer, so the windows are open, and a huge rotary fan is going overhead. I step closer and see that Gene and the other draftsmen are drawing bomb casings.

"Well, of course I remember Pearl Harbor," my mother says on my tape, the tone of her voice adding, "What do you think I am, an idiot?" She and my grandmother were working in my grandmother's dressmaking shop when they heard on the radio that the Japanese had bombed Pearl Harbor. She was five months pregnant with me. It was a Sunday. They'd never heard of Pearl Harbor. "It was out around Hawaii, in that part of the world, I guess." They knew it was serious, but they didn't think they were getting involved in a world war.

> There was another war going on south of Russia. Now which war that was, I don't know. Like every other thing, the conflict was so far away. We knew about it, and we heard it on the radio, but it didn't register to the point that it was . . . We just thought, oh, those Japs over there are fighting somebody, you know. Didn't make any difference. But as it went on, and spread, and all that type thing, and then they sent our boys to Hawaii and then on and out into the Pacific, then people got concerned. But really, the war didn't touch little towns like Wheeling.

What on earth is she talking about? Of course the war touched little towns like Wheeling. It touched everybody. But that unfocused reaction to the war and her disclaimer of any involvement in it is typical of my mother—indicative of the distance she felt from nearly all of the great affairs of the world. One of the roles she had learned to play superbly well was that of the "dumb little thing"—as she occasionally referred to herself. It would have been an easy role to pick up as a girl growing up in the teens, as the youngest, the baby in the family. "Dumb little things" aren't ever quite sure who is fighting whom, where, and for what purpose. Playing the dumb little thing would have appealed to men, would have appealed to Gene.

He probably thought of her as many men did of their wives—as "the little woman"—in her case, an accurate description. He probably liked it when *the little woman* played *the dumb little thing*; he would have seen her as cute and feminine. "Dictatorial" she called him.

> I couldn't take his, "You do this, this way, no other way." I had worked since I was sixteen, and here I was in my thirties, and I wasn't about to have anyone tell me what to do. I knew I could make a living, and no way was I going to kowtow to him. And he expected it. He was of the old, I guess, French background that he was the boss, the head of the house. But he ran into a snag when he married me.

Unlike most other Americans, Gene would remember the last years of the Depression as not bad at all. He'd never been unemployed. He hadn't been making much money, but he'd always had enough. *If you watch your pennies, you can get by on next to nothing,* I imagine him trying to tell his wife. It didn't matter how hard the times were, you could always find a dollar here, and another one there, to put away in the bank. Any little extra you picked up for teaching or performing—well, it all added up. Ten pennies make a dime, and ten dimes make a dollar.

Folks in the Depression had needed brightening up, and Gene had done his best to oblige them. Every chance he got, he mounted the stage himself, as a singer, a comic, a tap dancer, a clown. Wheeling Steel had even *paid him* to stage shows—how lucky could a man get in the middle of a depression? But in Hot Springs, no one was paying him to stage shows. There was a war on now. There were no more shows to be staged and no more kids to be taught to dance.

At forty-one, Gene's too old to be in the war, but he's doing war work, and he's proud of it. He and the other men in the engineering department follow the war the way American men always follow wars—exactly the way they follow baseball. They feel themselves part of a something far bigger than their individual lives. They share a sense of purpose, of dedication, that carries them day to day. They're doing men's work. They're going to beat those goddamn sneaky Japs at their own game. But then Gene comes home from that comradely, masculine, *satisfying* environment to find a wife who doesn't give a damn about the war. He's dog tired, trapped with a moody woman who can't see any farther than the walls of the house where she's living—who can't talk about anything but *the baby*.

I had been born prematurely, had always been underweight, had never lived up to the expectations on the doctors' charts, but it was in Hot Springs where I really started to go downhill. I might have been suffering from what we'd now call "failure to thrive syndrome," but then they just called me "sickly." I was supposed to be eating soft baby foods, but anything my mother fed me flowed straight through me and out the other end. Instead of gaining weight, I was losing it. She was worried to death. She must have been afraid that I was on my way out.

I watched her all the time. I didn't sleep as much as other babies. Sometimes I cried just like other babies, but I also went for long periods when I didn't cry. Wherever I lay, I followed her with my eyes. I seemed to be watching everything.

My mother had always been the baby in the family, but now she *had* a baby. She didn't have a clue what to do with a baby. My grandmother had made it seem so easy. She'd been there the day I was born. She would have been there, too, when I came home from the hospital. She would have shown my mother how to change diapers, how to give me a bottle, how to lay me down properly in my crib so I didn't suffocate in my sleep. As long as my mother had been in Wheeling, she could have picked up the phone and there, on the other end of the line, would have been her reliable, helpful, comforting mother who knew everything there was to know about babies. But now my mother was in Hot Springs, and it might as well have been out around Hawaii along with Pearl Harbor— that's how far away it felt. She wrote to her mother every day, but it took a week to get an answer back, and, good Lord, in a week, the baby could have died.

Alone with a baby. Every minute feels like an hour. What if he *is* dying? My mother believes the same thing that Gene believes— that everyone believes—that every woman knows how to be a mother. But she looks inside herself and can't find anything telling her how to be a mother. She doesn't know what to do. There's no one to ask. She's desperately afraid. What if she's the worst thing a woman could possibly be—a bad mother?

One afternoon when I was taking a nap, my mother stepped into the room to see how I was doing and saw a scorpion in my crib. I was asleep. The scorpion was not more than an inch from my cheek.

My mother could never tell this story without a shudder of horror and revulsion passing visibly through her entire body. In my recorded account, she runs out of words and utters a chilling high-pitched wail. The damned thing must have been, as I discover now, a striped bark scorpion, common to Arkansas. It would have been attracted to the moisture of my breath. An adult would have been about two-and-a-half inches long with a tail of a particularly nasty, putrescent yellow—except for the stinger, which would have been dark brown or black. My mother did not know the name of the scorpion. There are no scorpions in Wheeling, West Virginia. She had never seen a scorpion in her life.

The sting of the striped bark scorpion is hardly ever lethal, but my mother did not know that. I was an underweight infant, and maybe it could have killed me. My mother was utterly certain that it would kill me. As horrified and repulsed as she was, there was only one thing she could do, and she did it instinctively and instantly. She slapped the scorpion with the back of her hand and knocked it across the room. Then she grabbed me up from my crib, settled me safely on the couch in the living room, and hurried back to look for the scorpion. She knew she had to kill it. She stripped the bedding out of the crib and shook it. She looked behind drapes and under blinds and in dark corners and in the back of the closet. She went through every inch of that room. She didn't leave a single object unmoved or unturned. She never found the scorpion.

By his own lights, no one could ever accuse Gene of being a bad provider. He was doing his best for his family. "I need some help," Aileen had said, so he'd hired a local woman. Neither "mammy" nor "maid" were words my mother ever used; my mother called her, simply, "the help." In my mother's stories "the help" is as much of a stereotype as anything from a 40s movie—a culturally constructed image so seamless and opaque that I can't see behind it.

"I'd look out the window," my mother told me, "and here comes this big black lady." She wore high, black, lace-up shoes and carried a black umbrella to ward off the summer sun. She walked to my parents' house every morning, folded the umbrella, leaned it against the wall on the porch, unlaced her shoes, took them off, arranged them neatly by the umbrella, and worked the entire day barefoot. As soon as she stepped into the house, she got out the flour and baked a batch of biscuits. She baked biscuits for breakfast, lunch, and dinner. My mother would say, "That's very nice, thank you. But, please, don't bake any more biscuits."

"Yes, 'um," the help said. In my mother's reports, that's the main thing she said. My mother's instructions had no effect whatsoever. The biscuits continued to appear for breakfast, lunch, and dinner. My mother threw them out by the dozen. My mother hated biscuits for the rest of her life. When I was growing up, I never even *saw* a biscuit until I was in high school and eating dinner at a friend's.

Doctors in the 40s believed that babies should be trained to fit into a predetermined schedule. The doctor who'd delivered me in Wheeling had given my mother just such a schedule, and she was doing her best. The help knew better. She held me constantly. She rocked me and never put me down. My mother would say, "Don't do that. Put him in his crib."

"Yes, 'um," the help would say. She'd put me in my crib. My mother would go in the other room. When my mother came back, the black lady would always have picked me up again.

My mother would have known nothing about the help. She would never have attempted a conversation with her. By the time she told me the stories, she'd forgotten her name. From the experiences of a lifetime in Hot Springs, Arkansas, the help lady would have learned to play dumb even better than my mother, but I imagine her going home at night, saying to her husband, or her own kids, "That white lady don't know the first thing about babies." When a baby cries, you pick it up.

Help or no help, my mother was desperate. She had to talk to somebody. She heard from some of the other wives about an old doctor they all swore by, a pediatrician, so she went to see him. She had me in a diaper, and a t-shirt, and a romper, and shoes and socks, and a sweater. She'd even wrapped me in a blanket. The doctor was a large dignified man with a head of thick snow-white hair. He spoke as everyone did—in that slow southern drawl that grated on my mother's nerves. In no time flat he had me stripped down to the buff. He poked at the front of me with his finger, turned me over and poked at my back. "Mrs. Maillard," he said, "you've got too much clothes on this baby. It's the middle of the summer, for heaven's sake. *Never* put that many clothes on him. Don't put anything on him but a diaper."

My mother always laughed when she told this story—laughing at herself, at the dumb little thing she had been—but at the time, it wasn't the least bit funny. "Take him home and give him mashed bananas," the doctor told her. "Feed him as much as he can eat all day long."

Anywhere, Arkansas—your backwoods cracker existence is over. There's a war on, and every able-bodied male between the ages of eighteen and thirty has been sucked out of the population. The big bucks have arrived, courtesy of the United States Government. Every able-bodied female has a job if she wants one, but she's got to leave home to get it. Farms are abandoned. Kids are left behind. Appalled, the older folks are writing letters to the editor. The war has brought a "boom in badness," they're saying. Professional ladies are piling up in the hotel rooms in Little Rock. Women with honest jobs are strutting around town in high heels and slacks. Under-age boys are roaming the state in gangs, making a nuisance of themselves, breaking into folks' homes. Worst of all are the teenage "victory girls" who are doing their patriotic best to "improve the morale" of our boys in uniform—and picking up a little hard cash for their efforts. The rates of syphilis and gonorrhea are skyrocketing—my God, it's an epidemic! The authorities in Hot Springs do what everybody else in the state is jawing about but nobody else has the guts to do. They impose a curfew to keep those damnable teenagers off the street at night.

Trains are rolling into Hot Springs at all hours—dumping sick and wounded servicemen, carrying away the ones who've recovered. The Army has already taken over the immense Eastman Hotel, is in the process of gobbling up the smaller hotels on Bathhouse Row. None of the hustling, overheated, jammed up, chaotic human mess of Hot Springs has carried over into my mother's stories, but that alien world must have pressed in on her from all sides. She's trying to buy bananas. I will set this scene in the farmer's market I remember from my childhood—a long barn of a building with stalls running along both walls. My mother, pushing me in a carriage, has to maneuver through a million damned southerners. She's staring into stall after stall of fruit and vegetables. She can't find a single banana.

A tune that had been all the rage the year my mother was twelve must surely have been rattling in her brain—*YES, we have no bananas!* Corn, beans, potatoes, carrots, tomatoes, lettuce, even rutabagas—but no bananas. Apples, berries, melons, maybe even oranges from Florida—but no bananas. Hot Springs is a demonic puzzle, a hell hole that breeds scorpions but no bananas. She'd searched for the scorpion for hours. Her baby is dying, and she can't find bananas.

Defeated, she goes back to the doctor. He laughs at her. "The bananas you're used to . . . those long yalla things? That's not the way they are down here. Our bananas are short and green."

My mother mashed the short, green, stubby, alien bananas and fed them to me. When she couldn't take any more bananas or any more baby, she told the help to feed them to me. The effect was immediate. My body must have been crying out for starch and potassium. I gained weight. I slept through the night. Gene complained about the doctor's bill. "He told you to feed him bananas?" I imagine him saying. "*That's* what I'm paying for? And I'm paying him again because he had to tell you *what they look like.* Good Lord, Aileen, where's your common sense?"

"Gene and I used to walk downtown," my mother told me, "not to buy, no, to *look*. And anything that I needed, like a pair of shoes for you, we had to go to four different places, price them, look at the material, what they were made of, see if they were any good, then go home and compare, and then buy the best value. I never could go anyplace and buy it right now, and that drove me crazy. I was used to my own money, to going downtown. If I liked that, I bought it, no questions asked, it was *my* money. But not with Gene Maillard."

Many couples argue themselves into a single fight around which everything else revolves, a fight they keep having over and over again. If my parents had a fight like that, it was surely about *the money*. When it came to *the money*, my parents didn't merely have a difference of opinion; they had bitterly opposed worldviews. "Gene thought I was the most extravagant person he ever saw," my mother told me, shaking her head in amazement that anyone could think that of her.

There were things from steaks to television sets that we simply couldn't afford. We didn't think about "such foolishness," as my grandmother put it. What on earth could Gene have objected to about my mother? It couldn't have been any particular extravagant purchase. It must have been her attitude. He would have sensed instantly that she didn't think the way he did.

To my mother, money was filthy lucre. Disreputable and slimy, it was both absolutely necessary and absolutely disgusting. She would have preferred to live in a world in which money was handled by someone else—a man, of course—where it was never discussed. Only the lowest of the low would mention money. When an exact figure came out of anyone's mouth—the $25 for a suit or $5,000 for a house—you knew immediately that such a person was far down on the social ladder, beneath your contempt. That attitude, of course, was the Sharp talking. Money was supposed to mysteriously appear and take care of things—although we know that it doesn't, and so did my mother. For those seven years in the Depression the money is what had got her out of bed every

morning and sent her off to a blueprint shop to do the work she
hated. After she left Gene, she would never have money in the
bank; she would have debts.

But Aileen always had her moments when the Sharp in her just
had to get out. As broke as we were when I was growing up, she
could suddenly decide that we were going out to dinner and then
to a show—because sometimes you just had to do things like that
or life wasn't worth living. When she was old, she was a sucker for
weird gadgets advertised on television, would buy them on impulse
and send them to me—a specially lined ice tray that popped out
cubes at a touch, huge steel nails you drove though potatoes to
make them bake faster.

How did the money get to be so powerful and disgusting? The
money was what could have sent her to college and given her an
entirely different life, but didn't, because the father she adored—
openhanded and generous and carefree as always, as a Sharp should
be—threw it away in a poker game. That was both the upside and
downside, the angel and the demon of a man. A man could piss the
money away like P.A. or Bill, or he could spend it lavishly on you.
If Gene had wanted to keep her, he should have lavished his money
on her. If he'd been able to do that, she might well have been at
his bedside when he died at nearly ninety-six. But he was no more
capable of lavishing his money on her than she was of saving the
milk in the cereal bowl to use the next morning.

Gene's view of money was entirely different. In Gene's mind,
money was life itself. It was the difference between eating and
not eating, going to school and not going to school, making
something of yourself or being stuck in poverty your whole life,
chasing one job or another from pillar to post like a glassblower.
If money is life, then the worth of your life can be directly
measured by the amount of money you've got in the bank. If you
carry this notion to its logical extreme, then the money in the

bank is not something that you would want to spend—it's the way to keep score.

Gene would have known that Aileen was not playing his game and had no interest in learning to play it. He would have lied to her automatically, made himself out to be poorer than he was. He would never have allowed her to see his financial records. She was a trained and efficient bookkeeper, and there's no way she would have missed the little hoard that was already starting to pile up in the bank.

They're out one afternoon, pushing me in the baby carriage, not shopping but looking, and here comes the famous story of the nickel for a Coke. "Go home and drink water. It's free," he says. To deliver that line, you have to be pissed off—and not just about the nickel. You have to have been pissed off for so long that the nickel is the goddamned last straw—the latest beat in the ancient, interminable, irresolvable, and utterly maddening *fight*.

That's one way to play it. Here's another. Yes, he is annoyed, but he's trying to make a joke of it. "Come on, Aileen," he says with a laugh and a grin, "Go home and drink water. It's free." The joke's on her, on her extravagant ways, but it's on him too, an admission that he is—well, maybe just a little bit too tight with his money. How could she not get the joke? Nobody could say something like that and mean it.

No, that doesn't feel right. Okay, let me try it another way. Maybe he is trying it as a joke, delivers his line with a laugh, but it turns out to be one of those jokes we make all the time without understanding what we're doing—a joke that isn't really a joke, a joke with a stinger attached. The moment it's out of his mouth, he realizes how it must have sounded. He's appalled at himself but can't think of a damn thing to say that might fix it.

But no, I can't believe that version either. It wasn't a joke. I've

finally caught up to him. I know him well enough by now to feel
the fire of his outrage—to feel it burn in me too. It's a hell of a lot
bigger than the nickel for a Coke.

What does she know about it? Did she ever go without eating
because there was nothing to eat? Did she ever have to walk the
neighborhood with her stomach aching, so hungry she was ready
to kill, humiliating herself, begging "Excuse me, can I sweep your
porch? Shovel your coal? Can I do *anything*?" He's doing his best
to be a good husband, a good father, to provide for his family. If she
was a good wife, she wouldn't just take it for granted and piss the
money away. She'd help him, count the pennies right along with
him. That's what a good wife does. That's what his mother used to
do. The most important thing he has to teach his son is the value
of money, and if she was a good mother, she'd understand that.

The nickel for a Coke—he's said it, and he can't take it back.
Gene and Aileen can't do anything but keep on walking—in an
oppressive silence so loaded with subtext that we, the audience,
become acutely aware of the squeaky wheels of the baby carriage.
The camera dollies back slowly to give us a longer and longer
shot—as the doomed couple is lost among the crowd of shoppers
on that Saturday afternoon in 1942 in Hot Springs, Arkansas.

If my mother's official statement about the end of their marriage
blamed *the money*, Gene's official statement—his summary worked
out years later—blamed my grandmother, or, as he put it, *the
mother-in-law*, a standard butt of jokes in those days. In Gene's
accounts, my grandmother is always standing in the background,
one hefty arm upraised, clutching, not a rolling pin, as a cartoon
mother-in-law would, but a carving knife. That was the demonic
figure that Gene presented to his friends and Masonic brothers, the
reason his marriage failed, and there's a grain of truth to it.

Except for the years when she was married to Gene, my mother lived with her mother her entire life. Hot Springs was not merely strange, alien, incomprehensible, and scorpion-ridden; it was far from her mother. She wrote to her mother every day and expected a letter back every day. If she didn't get one, she'd call her long distance, running up Gene's phone bill. Aileen was *alone with a baby* and needed all the help she could get from the only person who could give it to her. She also felt guilty—as though she'd abandoned her mother. "I worried about her not having enough. I'd been with her all my life, and I knew she was staying up until midnight trying . . . putting that last stitch in something to earn a dollar, and I just couldn't stand it."

Gene may never have voiced the question, "Do you want to live with your mother or do you want to live with me?" but it must have been playing constantly in his mind.

It seems sad to me that the black lady who helped out my mother has lost her name but a walk-on character with one line of dialogue has retained hers. A young couple was living across the street from my parents. The wife's maiden name had been Schellenberg so her nickname was Shelly. "If her husband said jump, she jumped three times," my mother told me. "I don't know whether all southern girls are like that or not. They were back then. The man ruled the roost. But I'd worked too long for that. Hmm."

Shelly Fraser said to my mother, "You know what's wrong with your marriage? Your husband's more in love with you than you are with him."

If that was Shelly's invitation to southern girl talk, my mother wasn't having any. "That's none of your business," she snapped at her.

Shelly must have hit a nerve. My mother was feeling that sickening, claustrophobic, trapped sense of guilt we get when people love us more than we love them. She couldn't always have hated Gene Maillard's guts; at times she must have thought, *Oh, poor Gene.* She wanted to retain something of her independence, but she also wanted to be a good wife. As everybody knew then, a man has needs and a good wife satisfies her husband's needs.

I imagine Gene looking at his wife and thinking, *Oh, my God, why her?* He'd never had trouble getting girls; he could have married almost anyone else, but he'd chosen Aileen, and he was still trying to make the marriage work. He doesn't know why, but he loves her—and she's the mother of his son, and he wants a family. I imagine them in bed—his desperation. She puts up with him because that's what a good wife does. But he keeps asking something of her with his body—*Look at me, make me the center of your life. I'm your husband. Love me.* Night after night it gets more mechanical and desperate. She's drifting farther and farther away. He can feel her going.

The things that we know deep in our bones—the things that our entire life and experience have trained us to know—carry an absolute conviction. Gene knows, at that deep level, that we can be moved unexpectedly from town to town, that people in our lives can come and go, that even the people we love can be here one day and gone the next, but in the midst of that terrible flux and uncertainly, there's one thing that's stable, one thing we can always trust, and that's the money.

My mother knows, at that same deep level, that there is only one person she can trust, the one person who's been there forever, the one person who's never let her down and never will—her mother. She also knows that any man she loves will betray her, and when he does, it will be about the money.

Were my parents living in Hot Springs together only a few months or for as long as a year? How old was I, exactly, when she left him? I was wearing shoes—my mother and Gene had shopped for them—but you can put shoes on a baby before he can walk. My mother's stories have only one season attached to them—the oppressive heat of the Arkansas summer. At the height of the summer, I would have been six months old. When we boarded the train that would carry us away from there, I was old enough to eat mashed bananas but still drinking formula from a bottle. Did she leave him before my first birthday or after it? Exact dates might matter to me, trying to write about it, but they don't matter to my mother. For her, Hot Springs is a mythic time that lasts longer than anything that can be measured on a calendar. Hot Springs will always be there, as big as it needs to be, re-creating itself continually in an eternal present—until dementia eats up her memory.

The bananas have done the trick. I am eating. I'm getting bigger. She can see the pink coming into my cheeks. I'm sleeping better. But she's traded places with me. The blazing summer sun turns the house into a fetid steam bath. It reeks of baby shit, ammonia from the diaper pail, and alien mashed bananas. The stench makes her sick. There's nowhere she can go to get away from it—because she can't leave the baby. She keeps throwing away plate after plate of biscuits—and that might be funny someday, but it's not funny now. She can't eat anything. She can't keep anything down. She can't even imagine anything she might want to eat. She's losing weight. She can't sleep. Any pillow or blanket or shadow might have a scorpion under it.

My mother has no support. Her mother and her sister are far away. Shelly across the street has tried to include her in the wives' network, but my mother—proud, private, stubborn, and convinced that she, as a Sharp, is better than most people—shut her down before she'd even got started. My mother knows that she can't keep running back to the doctor—Gene would have a fit. The one person in her life who understands babies is arriving every morning, taking off her shoes and walking in barefoot, but it would never occur to Aileen to talk to her.

My mother gets up in the night and cleans the house again. She looks in every dark corner, pokes into the back of every cupboard and closet. This doesn't have any words. She can feel it in her stomach all the time. It never lets up. She can't think straight, and it scares her to death.

"There's a war on," Gene says. She knows that. Who does he think she is? She can't talk to Mother, tell her how bad it is. She says to herself that she doesn't want to worry her, but it's more than that. Keith may be doing okay for now, but for how long? What if he gets sick again? What if she doesn't put him down right and he dies in his sleep? What if *anything*? She can't take her eyes off the baby for a minute, and she can't talk to Gene. He's *a man*, what would he know? If the measure of a man is his money in the bank, the measure of a woman is how well she does as a mother. Everybody knows that motherly instincts are something you're born with, so she knows she's a failure. She can't admit that to anyone, not now and not ever.

One day, when Gene's at work, she calls her sister, Martha. She finds the only words she will ever be able to say about Hot Springs—"I can't live like this."

"Well, for Pete's sake, Aileen, you don't have to live like that. You'll come to my house. I'll get you and Keith back on your feet, and then I'll drive you to Wheeling."

Many pieces of this story I heard so many times that they became worn smooth as old banisters. The help is holding me on her lap, rocking me. Big tears are rolling down her cheeks. "Oh, please," she says, "don't take my baby away from me."

How it ended was something I heard only once. I'm certain that my mother had no intention of telling me, but every day while I was interviewing her, I pointed her in that direction. I did it as methodically and coldly as a cop interrogating a witness. At the end of the fourth day her unquenchable anger thrust her back nearly sixty years, right into the heart of it. "Well, Gene, I'm leaving you," she said to him.

I have to set the scene somewhere, so I'll put them in the kitchen. It's night, and the help has gone home. I'm asleep in my crib. Aileen is sitting in a kitchen chair. As I imagine it, Gene, who never raised his voice, gets even quieter. "I can't live like this," she's saying to him. "I wasn't raised like this."

In the scene I'm writing, my father has just stood up. To distance himself, he's leaning against the wall. To hold himself in, he's folded his arms across his chest. He's heard her say things like this before, so his first impulse is to make a joke of it, but then he guesses that would be crazy, so he stops himself. She's mad as a hornet, and everything he says, or tries to say, just makes matters worse. He's been watching this go on for a long time now. It's almost as bad as standing by, helplessly, and watching his father, and then his mother, die. Maybe he says, "Come on, Aileen, tomorrow's another day." A crushing hopelessness settles onto him. Nothing he says is ever right.

I've seen my mother in a fury. Her huge blue eyes freeze into a rigid stare. Her voice goes as bitter as vinegar. She makes a small smacking sound with her lips—a nasty click—rolls her eyes up at the ceiling, then focuses them again on my father's eyes. Now that she's leaving him, taking the baby home to her mother, she's not afraid—not even slightly. She doesn't have to take any more of his crap—she's *a Sharp*. Everything civil, gentle, domesticated about her drops away. All that's left is the icy clarity of her outrage.

Gene can't stand looking at her. He turns away, searches for words. When he speaks, his voice is so stifled he can barely hear himself. Maybe he says, "We'll get through this, Aileen." Maybe he says, "It's rough on everybody. There's a war on."

It's driving her up the wall—Gene's quiet, his control, and then his *silence*. How can he just stand there like that, the dictatorial son of a bitch? He's patronizing her again, treating her like the little woman again. Doesn't he get it? She has to make sure that he gets it. She can hear her own voice—loud, emphatic, dripping with sarcasm—and she lets the seductive power of it carry her. Everything she says is meant to cut to the quick.

Gene is beginning to get it. He's baffled, at the end of his rope. She's not kidding this time. She's made plans. She's got it all worked out. She's *got the money*. She's talked to her sister, talked to her *goddamned mother*. Long distance. God knows what those calls must have cost.

She's pushed him right to the limit. He's compromised and compromised and done his best, but he's gone as far as he can, and he's not going to give another inch. She went and named the baby Keith when he was working out of town—pure spite. He's thinking of his father now. Sometimes when he's drifting off to sleep, he can still hear Papa's breath rasping in that back bedroom. His son was supposed to be named Eugene. To honor Papa. My God, Aileen doesn't understand a damned thing.

Now I don't have to imagine what they said because this is what she told me. When I first heard it, I imagined them yelling at each other, but now, having written my way here, I don't think so. Gene finds his voice again. It's clear and hard, but he's not yelling. "You'll never get a penny."

My mother's not yelling either. She's simply stating the facts, the way it's going to be, now and forever. "You'll never know him."

That trip back from Hot Springs . . . It was a troop train. They were transporting troops. I was lucky to get on that train. They had one car with seats, train seats in it, and it was like a special car. You had to pay twice as much for the fare, and they gave me a little

compartment of a bed and a toilet in this little room that wasn't
any bigger than right here. And that's where I was, but no food.
You were hungry, and you started to cry. They, ah . . . they moved
the train onto a side track so this long troop train could go past,
and there we sat, and we were supposed to get into Cincinnati
hours before. And there we sat. And sat. And you were hungry,
and you started screaming.

They were all sitting on the floor. All these fellas. With their
backs up against each other and their legs . . . But anyhow, and
this tall southern fella, a soldier, knocked on the door, and he
says, "Wha . . . Is your baby hungry?"

I said, "Yes."

He says, "I have two of my own." He says, "Bring him . . ." or
"Give him to me." He reached down, and he picked you up, and
he took my hand, and he says, "Catch ahold of my belt and don't
let go."

He went through that troop train—I was right behind him—
to the kitchen, and he says, "We need some milk."

The chef, or the man in charge, says, "Nope. Nobody gets
milk."

He says, "I want some milk for this baby!"

And the man turned around . . . looked at him, looked at you,
and he gave it. And you had been on a dumb formula all your life.
You didn't drink cow's milk. But that's what he gave us, and that's
what I gave you, and you drank it. Oh, dear.

Martha and Harley met me in Cincinnati, and they had
waited hours. I remember seeing Martha. I had you, and you
were . . . I was exhausted. All I did when I got off the train
was take you and hand you to Martha. I don't remember much
from then on. Harley caught ahold of me and got me through
the . . . wherever we were to the car, and I just passed out. I
handed you to Martha, and Harley put his arm around me,

and I don't remember anything else till I got awake in College Corner in bed.

Martha was appalled. She called Mother. I remember hearing her. Says, "Well, we got her. And she's here. And I'm going to keep her for two or three weeks," and Mother must have asked why, and Martha says, "Well, she's tired." She didn't go into it. But I had lost so much weight because I couldn't eat. Martha was mighty good to me . . . and Harley. He was putting the money out. I was in bed two weeks out at Martha's. And she took care of you. The doctor . . . he was a friend of theirs . . . he says, "Just let her sleep. If she gets awake, give her some soup." Lord, Keith, I only weighed seventy-nine pounds.

I could end this story with Aileen lying in bed at Martha's, watching the light fade out at the window, as she listens to Martha talking to my grandmother long distance, telling her, "Well, she's tired." I could imagine myself somewhere in Martha's house, crying or sleeping. But I've told those stories before, and this time I'm going to stay with Gene. I'd always known that my mother had been devastated by Hot Springs, but Gene was just as devastated. He's thinking, "Well, there she goes, Gene, with your son. Three strikes and you're out."

23.

"YOU KNOW WHAT?" J.R. SAYS, "we've spent all this time and energy thinking about him, trying to figure him out, but he might not have given a damn about us."

"It's true," I say, laughing.

My brother and I are lounging in the outdoor hot tub, taking turns blasting our tired muscles with the water jets we've turned up to full force. It feels great. The sky overhead is beginning to slide toward the pewter-gray of evening. Still following his line of thought, J.R. says, "We might have turned up, and he might have said, 'What do you guys want from me? Come on, get out of here. I don't want to know you.'"

For most of my life I would not have found that possibility funny, but I find it funny now. "You're absolutely right. I don't think we could ever have convinced him that we weren't after his money."

The soaring dot in the sky above me circles down and reveals itself to be the eagle that lives in the tree by our balcony. We're on vacation, and this is a house we've rented for a week in Tofino on Vancouver Island. My daughters are wandering around somewhere, radiating the day's sun, nattering at each other in an ongoing sisterly conspiracy. They're probably planning to slip out later, after dinner, to check out what there might be of a night life in this coastal town where they're sure to find beer and boys. My wife is doing what she likes to do best; inside, lounging on a couch by the broad expanse of window, she's reading a book, looking up from time to time to take in the view of the sky and sea. And it strikes me that J.R. and I are like characters in a comedy routine entitled "Two Old Guys in a Tub." Our years have earned us the right to amuse ourselves any way we damned well please. We don't talk about Gene Maillard all the time, but this seems like a good time to talk about him.

The money—the core of the story. "He spent the larger part of his working life helping to make things that kill people." I say. "Maybe that's why he wanted his money to go to good causes . . . like old Nobel, the guy who invented dynamite, endowing the Nobel Peace Prize . . . Do you think that's possible?"

"No," J.R. says, "I don't think it ever crossed his mind."

The beaches at Tofino stretch the ruler-straight horizon to infinity. That afternoon we walked so far that we were moving dots to each other, our long lines of footprints in the sand linking us like afterthoughts. Now, with the jets of water pounding the muscles below my shoulder blades, I have the sensation of living inside my body in a way that tells me how much of the time I don't. J.R. and I are grinning at each other. We were not supposed to meet. The script had been written for us long before we ever stepped onto the scene. But here we are in spite of it, and we've survived all manner of dubious shit to get here—Gene's two wandering unacknowledged sons.

"I'm not sure where my home is," I say to him. "Do you ever feel like that? I miss West Virginia . . . love that crazy state. I go back every chance I get, and I always have a great time, but if I stay there long enough, I always start missing Vancouver. Then when I come back here, I write another story set in West Virginia. How do you feel about Santa Fe? Does it feel like home to you?"

"It feels more like home than anywhere else, but . . ." He laughs again. "Maybe you and I don't have a home."

A couple of months later J.R.'s back in Santa Fe, and I'm back in Vancouver. My daughter and I have just carried dozens of cartons and file boxes downstairs and into the garage for storage—masses of notes, census records, letters, pictures, sundry memorabilia, half a dozen drafts of this manuscript, and my father's scrapbooks. For the first time in years I have empty space in my closet and on the floor in front of my bookshelves. "So are you done with him?" Liz asks me.

"Well, yeah, pretty much. I still have to fiddle with the writing, but you always have to fiddle with the writing."

"Did you find out everything you wanted to know?"

"Oh, yeah, I guess so. Some periods of his life, I could tell you what he was doing practically day to day. You go back and try to inhabit your parents' time, and . . ."

"Dad?" she says, interrupting me.

"Yeah?"

"I don't want to have to . . . Like I don't want to have to read your books to figure out who you were. I don't want to have to spend years going through a whole freakin' pile of shit, like all those papers and letters and scrapbooks and shit. I want to know who you are right now."

Still mulling over what Liz has just said to me, I'm walking on the ridge above my house, soaking myself in the brilliant hot sun and memories of high summer—July in West Virginia entwined into July in British Columbia—and feeling displaced, sprung out of time, decompressed and empty, my mind not doing much of anything, floating just at the edge of sadness.

I'm feeling the limitations of language. If writing is like blowing glass, then I've been blowing bottles to hold fireflies. Time passes and unwinds us out—in the twelve years since that lawyer called and told me that my father was dead, my daughters have grown up—and it's the vividness of life having become habitual that gives us the illusion of permanence. I've finally figured out what Liz meant. It's not that she doesn't want my handcrafted bottles—it's that she wants the fireflies.

Sun and heat, and I could walk out of this—the sense of being a visitor. The possibilities are all still here, just as clearly as they always have been, but what's sad is that we're running out of years. Being a father isn't so much about what you say—it's more a matter of *being there*. All kids, when they grow up, discover flaws in their parents, and I'm sure that my daughters have discovered flaws in me, but I swear that neither Jane nor Elizabeth will be able to say, "I never knew him."

24.

AMONG THE SACRED RELICS I retrieved from the display case in the Masonic Hall in Escondido, California, was the sheet music for Gene's song "Bounce" and his correspondence about it. A copy of Gene's original letter is not included, but Dave Dreyer, the General Professional Manager of the Irving Berlin Music Corporation, responded to it on October 15, 1946. Mr. Dreyer admits a similarity between Gene's song and Irving Berlin's but claims that the Berlin song, although copyrighted in 1946, is a rewrite of something that Mr. Berlin had originally written ten years earlier. He also informs Gene that he has looked over "Little Boy Brown Eyes," another song that Gene had submitted, presumably for sale, but "in as much as Mr. Berlin writes all the songs that we publish, it would be, of course, impossible for us to accept any outside manuscripts."

On October the 28th, 1946, an extremely piqued Gene wrote directly to Irving Berlin himself: "Here is a matter which I think should be brought to your personal attention. I have a number called 'BOUNCE' which melody is similar to your number called 'I'VE GOT THE SUN IN THE MORNING'—so much so that I've had to stop using my number just when I was getting a good start. I have a great twelve-piece orchestration that so far I've never been able to use due to the similarity between the two numbers." Gene points out that his tune was copyrighted one month before

Irving Berlin's. "From where I stand it looks like this constitutes an infringement."

"Mr. Berlin," he concludes, "I've written some twenty-five (25) numbers and have established a bit of prestige among my fellow musicians and composers, and I'd like to remove the stigma of suspicion that I have garnished the fruits of some other person's labor. The whole thing throws an unholy light on my composing and you could do me a great service if you could straighten out this whole matter."

Gene included the sheet music for Irving Berlin's "I've Got the Sun in the Morning" for storage in the Masonic display case along with his own tune "Bounce" as though inviting anyone—even me— to compare the two, so I did. Both are in the key of F and follow the conventions for pop songs of the day. Berlin's tune is supple and syncopated, appears, on the surface, to be simple but is actually quite sophisticated. Gene's tune, on the other hand, *is* simple. Except for a single note that Gene takes off the beat, his tune marches along on stiff quarter notes, but it's bright and cheerful.

The two melodies do not resemble each other most of the time, but there is a rising three-note figure that is identical in both. It would not take a musical genius to find that figure; anybody fooling around on a keyboard, resolving the dominant back to the tonic, could find it easily enough, but lean hard on those three notes—C, E, F—as both songs do, and, yes, for a moment, the songs sound alike. Someone probably did come up to Gene and say, "Hey, that sounds like that song from *Annie Get Your Gun*." But whatever Irving Berlin thought of Gene's letter, he did not reply.

Of Gene's twenty-five numbers, nineteen of them are listed by title in the Copyright Office of the Library of Congress. I don't have access to the sheet music, but I'd love to know what Gene had to say in the lyrics of "Happy Children," "Gee, What a Fix I'm In," "Chum, You Need a Wife," "I'm So Confused, What Can I

Do?" or, especially, "Little Boy Brown Eyes," the tune that he tried
unsuccessfully to sell to the Irving Berlin Music Corporation.
There were, of course, two little brown-eyed boys Gene might have
been remembering. One was still very much a little boy, living in
Wheeling, West Virginia, with his mother and grandmother. The
other was a teenager, living with his grandparents in Washington,
DC, where he had been dumped by his mother and his stepfather
as they'd gone sneaking off secretly to Florida to spend some time
alone together in the sun.

I do have the lyrics to "Bounce," and they interest me more
than the disputed melody. Gene is recommending his survival
tactic, telling us how to deal with our sorrows just as he has
always done:

> You will agree, come what you do,
> That life is what you make it!
> Don't let worries bother you,
> Make up your mind to shake it—So!
>
> Bounce your body, let it spring,
> While you sing a merry tune.
> Raise your voice, let it ring.
> You'll be feeling happy soon.
>
> Slap your thigh, keep in rhythm,
> Flex your knees and walk around.
> Shake your head, keep right with "em,"
> A new sensation you have found.
>
> Now you're "cookin," don't you hurry,
> "Lax" your body, let it spring.
> Never fret, never worry,
> All you have to do is sing.

Bounce your body, let it go,
While you sing a merry tune.
Slap your hands, don't you know,
You'll be feeling better soon.

And you'll live to be a hundred!

Gene didn't live to be a hundred, but he came close.

When Irving Berlin was not replying to his letter, Gene was halfway through his forties and living in Springdale, Pennsylvania, a town eighteen miles from Pittsburgh. He and I had already laid eyes on each other for what would turn out to be the last time in our lives. He was working at whatever job Sanderson & Porter had assigned him. He'd been promoted by then from draftsman to junior engineer, so he must have been making good money and stuffing as much of it as possible into the bank. His address was Box 8, so he must have been living alone in a boarding house or a rented room.

When I was halfway through my forties, I was living alone in a bachelor apartment near City Hall in Vancouver and drinking too much. I had just survived another busted-up relationship and knew that I was in no shape to try to start another one. My four published novels had brought me good reviews but no money. For my entire adult life I had defined myself as a writer, but at that point, the only writing I was able to do was jotting my dreams into a notebook, and I didn't count that as writing. I had abandoned my fifth novel. My editor—the most sympathetic and patient of men—was waiting for me to finish the damned thing so he could publish it, but I'd fucked it up so badly I couldn't stand to look at it. I'd lost the essential writer's compass that had always enabled me to tell the difference between good writing and bullshit. All writing—my own and everybody else's—looked equally crappy to me. I'd lost any sense of what my book was supposed to be about—of what *my life* was supposed to be about.

Sitting alone in his room writing to Irving Berlin, Gene must have felt just as bad as I did sitting alone in mine. His parents, grandparents, and two of his brothers were long dead. He had tried marriage three times and failed at each, leaving behind women who despised him. He had disowned what remained of his family. He had fathered two sons and had no plan to see either of them again. He had some songs to his credit, and a scrapbook full of memories—and, of course, the considerable consolation of his money in the bank. He would always have Masonic brothers and grateful students in his life, but never again that intimate, intense, responsible, enlivening human connection we call family—and he must have known that. He might even have chosen it. The man under the hat, under the hat, under the hat was a sad man—as clowns so often are.

But, as Gene was telling himself in his song, life is what you make it, right? Just because *I* wouldn't have chosen his life doesn't mean that there was anything wrong with his choice. It was *his* life, after all, and he was headed for that most apple-pie American of small towns—Richland, Washington—where there would be students to teach, shows to produce, lots of good people who would love him for the twinkle in his eye. The folks in Richland would be pulling together, helping each other out, building a town in a desert, and he'd be right there with them, cheering them on and brightening them up.

"Your dad was a good man, Keith," Kippy told me. She was right. When Gene was old, he wasn't talking about making weapons-grade plutonium. He was talking about those fabulous, magical, unforgettable nights when he and his students leapt onto the stage and knocked 'em dead.

Halfway through *my* forties, desperate for help, I rode the Greyhound down to Seattle for a weekend of intensive therapy. That's when my father surprised me by appearing in an empty chair. In the story I had always told myself, Gene had left me without a qualm, without a backward glance, riding blithely off into the sunset feeling not much of anything, but when I met him in Seattle, he was crying just as hard as I was.

The therapist guided me to Hot Springs, Arkansas, where my father said goodbye to me. My mother carried me onto the troop train. I screamed with hunger as we waited interminably on the siding, drank the milk supplied by the US Army, slept as we rode to Cincinnati, and woke again when my mother handed me over to my aunt Martha. Then the therapist guided me to my aunt's house where I was left alone in a guest room. I had just lost my father, the wonderful black lady who had taken care of me in Hot Springs, and my mother, who was collapsed in another room. The therapist was ramming me into a metaphor for utter abandonment, and it was just as effective as it was supposed to be—I was howling like an infant. She handed me a pillow and said, "This is little Keith. What do you want to say to him?"

Wholly inside the story, I took the pillow into my arms and felt it as a child. What on earth could I possible say to that crying child? But you don't talk to a small child, you comfort it. I pressed the pillow against my chest and had one of those powerful transformative insights you hope to achieve in therapy and actually do sometimes if you're lucky. Up until that moment I had told myself—and everyone else—that I never wanted to have children, but I'd been lying. I badly wanted to have children but had denied it because *I was afraid of being a father.*

While I was growing up, I listened in fascination when my buddies told me about their fathers, wishing that I had one. I've spent years learning as much as I could about Gene Maillard and trying to write a version of him I could believe. What I've found is a father much like theirs—neither an angel nor a demon. I admire him, and he infuriates me. He got some things right and other things disastrously wrong. I see through him straight to the heart, and he remains utterly incomprehensible to me. I hate the son of a bitch, and I've developed a deep affection for him. We're as different as two people could possibly be, and I'm enough like him that it scares the hell out of me.

I've got Gene's brown eyes, broad jaw, full-lipped mouth, and distinctive walk. He and I were both scrawny, underweight kids bedeviled with serious allergies and a multitude of other childhood illnesses. We both lost our fathers and were raised by women, grew up poor in West Virginia. We're clever, inventive, and drawn to the arts. We both became successful by doing things our own damned way and convincing other people that it was the right way. We're intractable loners and also, oddly enough, intensely social with a natural sympathy for other people. We're self-taught musicians who wrote songs, and we're both entertainers. We reconstructed ourselves. From our twenties on into middle age, we were always romantically involved with women, and we were both married three times, although my third marriage lasted and his didn't. I'm not as tight as Gene, but I feel the same niggardly impulse—spending money is genuinely painful to me. Both of us, when we had to choose, opted for a safe day gig instead of the drifting uncertain life of the artist. We were nomads, wandered far from home and ended up on the west coast, stopped by the sea.

Would Gene have liked me? Would I have liked him? I've come to see those questions as pointless. As any West Virginia boy knows, you don't have to like your relatives, but you're stuck with them because they're *your people*. My need to read Gene Maillard into my life was like a vacuum that continually drew stories into it—layer upon layer of intertwined stories of people and the places and histories and events. Wishing to leave me nothing, Gene, in spite of himself, left me the greatest gift I can imagine—stories to the storyteller. At its darkest center, absence was deeper than my father or his absence. It was a creative emptiness, shining and inexhaustible.

ACKNOWLEDGMENTS

MANY YEARS OF RESEARCH went into writing this book, and I want to thank everyone who talked or corresponded with me. Even though your name might not appear here, your contribution was invaluable. I conducted formal interviews—either written or recorded—with a number of people. In order of appearance they are: Gene's executor, Gus Klammer; Gene's former student, Kippy Lou Scott (née Brinkman); my cousin, Dr. Frank Wade; Kippy's father, Loris "Brink" Brinkman; my brother, J.R. (Robert) Maillard; my mother, Aileen Maillard (née Sharp); my first cousin, Eddie Maillard's daughter, June Dutton (née Maillard).

Kippy Lou Scott, who shared her stories of Gene, also taught my daughter Elizabeth one of Gene's tap routines and brought us Gene's record player and home music studio with the original records that he had made to teach his students.

Carolyn Ugolini, a superb professional genealogist in Salt Lake City, Utah, researched parish records in Bedonia and Compiano, Italy, and confirmed my grandmother Clementina Mariani's birth and family history.

Barbara Bulgarelli (née Vallee), the granddaughter of Elisa Vallee's sister, told us the story of Eugene F. Maillard bringing the body of his wife, Elisa Vallee, by train to Montreal from Indiana. Vallee family legend has it that composer Gussie Davis who wrote "In the Baggage Coach Ahead" was a porter on that train.

In 2003 we spoke with Pat Carmoney who told us fascinating stories about her mother Lynette Rose Cochrane and Lynette's mother Lucille Hanna. It was Lucille who suggested that her daughter Lynette had been pregnant with twins.

One of the joys of this fascinating journey was meeting so many new cousins. When our story began to loop back from Montreal to West Virginia, the first link was supplied by Elizabeth "Betty" Brunet, widow of my cousin Emile Brunet. Another cousin, Jim Tommasin of Eighty Four, Pennsylvania, shared with me remarkably vivid stories of his grandfather John Tommasini and his times. We were introduced to the Battié family by my cousin, Neil Battié, grandson of Louise Battié (née Maillard) of Joliette, Quebec. Then, from the friendly, chatty emails we exchanged with his sister, Dorice "Dodie" Battié of Mississauga, Ontario, we learned that the Canadian Maillards had stayed in touch with their Lyon, France, family well into the twentieth century. Dodie also told us that when Louis Maillard was killed by a runaway horse and buggy, he was returning home from a band practice.

In 2007, while we were visiting my first cousins "Sis" (Lily Eugenie Buchholz, née Maillard) and Laura Mae (McFadzen, née Maillard) in Chemainus, British Columbia, we put Sis on the phone with our cousin Jeanne Evans (née Brunet) in Follansbee, West Virginia. The last time they had spoken to each other had been 1926 when they had lived together under one roof in Follansbee. After they had talked for a few minutes, they both remembered the story of the burning of the fiery cross. When we were in Follansbee, Jeanne told us many family stories, corroborated many factual details, and gave us a copy of the 1900 photograph of the Maillard family in Montreal.

My cousin John Dutton and his wife Irene of Chemainus, British Columbia, and my cousins Carol Hendon of Follansbee, West Virginia, and Jim Inman and Cynthia Fleming of Wellsburg, West Virginia, graciously supported this writing project and helped to make it happen.

Except for correcting obvious misprints, I have not edited Eddie Maillard's three letters to his wife Aggie nor Louis Maillard's two letters to her. These documents are owned by Eddie's daughter, my cousin, Laura

Mae McFadzen (née Maillard). I have transcribed and published them here with her permission.

Many of the items in Gene's scrapbooks have neither a date nor a source attached. He gave interviews to two local newspapers: *The Columbia Basin News* in Pasco, Washington, February 2, 1963, and *The Times-Advocate* in Escondido, California, June 20, 1975. Both of these have ceased publication.

Chapter 22 first appeared, in slightly different form, in *Southern Cultures*, Fall 2011, under the title of "Hot Springs, Arkansas." The prose in the paragraph "Anywhere Arkansas" is mine. All of the information contained in that paragraph, however, comes from C. Calvin Smith's excellent book *War and Wartime Changes: The Transformation of Arkansas 1940–1945* (The University of Arkansas Press, 1986).

Two excerpts from *Fatherless* originally appeared in different form in the spring 2011 edition of the online journal *Numero Cinq*: "Kilroy: A Writer's Childhood" and "Richland." Both of these selections contain material that I have subsequently cut from this book.

Of the articles and books I read about glassblowing, one of the most useful and interesting was Dr. Frederick Barkey's *Cinderheads in the Hills: The Belgian Window Glass Workers of West Virginia* (The Humanities Foundation of West Virginia, 1988).

I want to thank John Pearce, my tireless agent; Rebecca Rider, my meticulous copy editor; and Abby Freeland and the rest of the WVU Press team who brought this book into the world. It is customary for writers to thank their husbands or wives at the ends of their books, writing such things as "I couldn't have done it without you." In this case, it's absolutely true. Thank you, Mary. I *couldn't* have done it without you. I couldn't even have *begun it* without you.

I wrote this book while I was a grateful guest on the unceded territory of the Squamish and Tsleilwaututh Nations.

Keith Maillard
February 28, 2019

CPSIA information can be obtained
at www.ICGtesting.com
Printed in the USA
JSHW010942200819
1107JS00008B/9

9 781949 199130